The Life and Times of
GOPAL KRISHNA GOKHALE

The Life and Times of
GOPAL KRISHNA GOKHALE

Mamta Kumari

Ocean Paperbacks

A Division of Ocean Books Pvt. Ltd.

ISO 9001:2008 Publishers

Published by
Ocean Paperbacks
A Division of Ocean Books Pvt. Ltd.
4/19 Asaf Ali Road,
New Delhi-110 002 (INDIA)
e-mail: info@oceanbooks.in

ISBN 978-81-8430-549-4
The Life and Times of Gopal Krishna Gokhale
by Mamta Kumari

Edition
First, 2018

Price
₹ 175.00 (Rupees One Hundred Seventy Five only)

Printed at
R-Tech Offset Printers, Delhi

Contents

Preface

Gopal Krishna Gokhale was born on 9 May 1866 at Kotluk village of Ratnagiri district in an ordinary family. He was a great freedom fighter, social servant, philosopher and reformist. Gopal Krishna, the student of Mahadev Govind Ranade, was called 'Gladstone of India', due to his unparalleled understanding of financial matters and capacity to discuss the same with authority. He was the most famous moderate-styled leader of Indian National Congress. In 1905, he established 'Servants of India Society', in agreement with character building so that youth can be trained for public life. He considered scientific and technological education as India's significant need.

Subordination and dependence of country kept on pinching Gopal Krishna. An eve flowing currently of patriotism always kept on running in his conscious mind. That is why he kept on working under the confluence of trishades of true zeal, faith and dutifulness.

Gopal Krishna, the worthy son of Mother India, will always be remembered for simplicity of his character and conduct, intellectual capability and long selfless service to the nation.

Dedication to Those Unknown Revolution asks, owing to whom we are breathing in a free India?

Introduction

Gopal Krishna Gokhale was born on 9 May 1866 at a place called Kotluk in Maharashtra in a Brahmin family. After acquiring graduation degree in 1884, Gokhale became the member of the society called 'Deccan Education Society', which was established by Justice Ranade. Gopal Krishna Gokhale, who was the pupil of Mahadev Govind Ranade, was entitled as 'Socrates of Maharashtra' and guide 'GURU' of Mahatma Gandhi also.

In 1888, Gokhale entered into the politics through Congress session at Allahabad. In 1897, as a member of 'Deccan Education Committee', Gokhale and Wacha were asked to bear testimony at 'Welby Commission' in England. In 1902, Gokhale was selected as a member of Imperial Legislative Council. He raised issues of assigning more seats into the government jobs, about salt tax, compulsory primary education in the council there.

An aggressive section criticised his patience very much. Often he was introduced as a relaxed liberal person, while on the other hand, the British Government called him an aggressive ideas' follower and a disguised rebel.

Gokhale was a nationalist also along with being a moderate. He used to consider devotion to English equal to patriotism. Gokhale could not dream of any progress in India possible without English empire. Thinking of ill-consequences of the challenging English empire made him a big supporter of English empire. Hardinge told Gokhale, "If English left India to more away from it, then Indian leaders will them via wireless to return even before British could reach their native country. The aggressive section called him a weak hearted, liberal and disguised disloyal. In 1905, he chaired the Congress session at Banaras and he cooperated to form '1909 Morley Minto Reform Act'. Gokhale remained as the Chairman of Indian Public Service Commission from 1912 to 1925. Gokhale established 'Servants of India Society', on 12 June 1905 to train national propagators for the service of the nation. P. Shrinivas Shastri, G.K. Deodhar, N.M. Joshi, Pandit Haridaya Nath Kunjru, etc. were prominent social servants coming from this society. Gokhale edited the magazine/journal of 'Pune Public Society' and he was also the editor of *Sudharak."*

Convassing 'Swadeshi' or indigenised goods, Gokhale supported industrialisation but was opposed to the policy of 'Boycott'. Though owing to his compromising nature, he supported the proposal of boycott in 1906 at Calcutta Congress session. Gokhale died in 1915.

Mahatma Gandhi said about his this political 'Guru', "Sir Firozeshah Mehta appeared like Himalaya to me, which cannot be scaled and Lokmanya Tilak did look like an ocean which none can fathom easily. But Gokhale was like the Ganges which calls out to everybody to it."

Tilak called Gokhale 'Diamond of India', 'Worthy Son of Maharashtra' and kind of workers bestowing praise on him.

This book is an attempt to throw light on the personality and accomplishment of Gokhale.

—Mamta Kumari

1

British Empire in India

The two-hundred-year-old British commercial company called East India Company was continuing in India. It gathered unlimited power through their business activities. India is a country of ancient civilisation but it's political condition was pitiable. Apart from the above mentioned company, the British Government was also there, which wanted to control this company because most often it's agents used to cross their limit and sometimes used to commit irresponsible acts. The British Government had acquired rights to appoint Governor-General and main political leaders itself so that it could control the above mentioned company's political activities under Lord North's 1773 Regulatory Act and Pitt's 1784 India Act.

India had a few independent local kings, some of whom were a little more ambitious, powerful and treated the company with animosity. Mysore's Tipu Sultan and few Maratha princes are specially mentionable. Besides these, there were also French people, who wanted to affirm their foothold in India and weaken British sovereignty over India. Both France and Britain were at war in Europe. Meanwhile, French people tried to remove British influence from India. Both France and Britain wanted to set their interest with the assistance of local kings. The authority, which was desired by both the competing European powers and in which Britain succeeded, that power or attempt was not only to gain authority but also to bring local princes or kings under their (Britain and France) indirect rule. Such a situation in India was almost difficult, unsystematic and tricky. But during this period, the increase in British influence ones India was product of this mess only. The rise of British Empire in India was the result of neither empire policy nor any well-planned ideas of the British Government. In fact, the British Government never ordered to establish the British Empire in India. Whatever its agents did or whatever was done in this direction, that was rather without the British Government's consent and is against the will of the British Government as well. There was even an Article in India Act of 1784, which prohibited occupation of any more states in India. But opposition was repeatedly shown against the situation of India in the British Parliament. Still then every Governor of India considered it extremely essential to establish the British Empire and nurse it to the fullest. The British Government wanted to maintain the prevailing arrangement only for the already established reign of the British Government. But the British officers working in India tried their best to cement their foothold of the British and the situation of Britain be strong and powerful.

Those officers manipulated deteriorating condition of Indian affairs and succeeded in making their European enemy, France's ambitions roll the dust.

Warren Hastings was the Governor of East India Company in India from 1772 to 1785. Ramsaymuir has termed him the, 'Greatest Britisher of the eighteenth century'. During freedom struggle of America, India's local princes/kings, their French friends, Haider Ali of Deccan and Maratha's leaders of north and central India tirelessly teamed up to pull out the British power from India into the ocean. Only Warren Hastings defended the British empire in India during this difficult situation. He established peaceful system in Bengal and reformed/

amended its administrative system with required steps. But on return to his native land, he filed a case on himself as a punishment. After Warren Hastings, from 1786 to 1792, Cornwallis was made the Governor of India. He was sent to India to fulfil the target lest aggressive policy employed for India should not get reducing. But even Cornwallis was compelled to follow his prevailing policy. He completed Warren Hastings' unfinished responsibility by reforming rule in Bengal. He had also to fight against power of Nawab Tipu Sultan of Mysore, as was done by Hastings. Tipu Sultan was the son of Haider Ali. This fight was won and this was the victory of Great Britain.

Lord Wellesley continued to be the Governor of India from 1798 to 1804. This was Wellesley only, who practically established the British empire in India. In 1798, when Lord Wellesley accepted his post in India, it was the most delicate period for the British rule in India. At that time, Napolean had arrived at the Gate of Egypt and, in this way, he arrived closer to India. Exactly, meanwhile, the French people got in complicity with the native kings in India. This way great danger was faced by British motives and interests but Wellesley dethroned Tipu Sultan – stripping him of his authority and later he disrupted even the Maratha power with the assistance of his younger brother, Duke of Wellington. He expanded British occupation in South and North-East of India and won over few new states in favour of the British Government. He was single-handedly responsible for totally crushed French ambitions ultimately and the French could never raise their head in India in future.

Lord Hastings remained the Governor of India from 1813 to 1823. He believed in progressive policy and considered India's welfare under British possession only. He abolished Maratha power forever and cemented firm foothold of the British empire. In this way, local mismanagement and French challenges to India and enmity to the British empire led to a huge Anglo-Indian empire. If Britain had got unable to face the challenges, then it would have to run away leaving the posts position it created, sculpted for self in India. Besides, this Britain would have to get stripped itself of Clive's success stories along the success of patient and tough struggle since the last two centuries. Accepting that challenge meant expansion of influence and empire. In 1785, when Warren Hastings bade India adieu, only Bengal State remained under the British rule – a coastal district called 'Sarkar' and presidencies of Madras (now Chennai) and Bombay (now Mumbai). But in a span of forty years, after 1785, Great Britain had occupied the entire 'Ganges Valley Region', except Awadh. Expanded land region of Marathas in central India may also almost entire south India.

It won't be improper to quote Lord Hastings' proud expression here – "These can be called my proud words but it is absolutely true that we have gifted pleasure and prosperity to crores of Indian citizens. Even during this short span of time, they have come out of such caves and deserted spots, where they were lying for years. Now they are arriving to their old deserted villages to toil in their fields. The deserted lands without ploughing since the last so many years and which were trampled by bloody soldier riders and horse hooves, the very same lands are ploughed today in a state of well-being by their old owner farmers." Even after this much, directors of East India Company were complaining of futility of British reign expansion in India.

During this period only, England won few states and land parts from France, while France did same to the allied nations, during French Revolution period. This was the fourth annexation of the British empire. The most profitable land was snatched from Holland. Holland gave up land area of Cape of Good Hope, Sri Lanka and Guyana. At that time, Cape of Good Hope, was considered as a strategically important station base on way of India but later it proved to be very precious foundation of the

British empire laid in South Africa on its basis only. Indian empire of Britain enhanced its grandeur with Sri Lanka and Britain also gained foothold in South America through the acquisition of Guyana. England also obtained certain other islands which were laying scattered here and there. Their utility was to serve as ports suitable for ship-halt there or expanded nearby empire of some big British sovereign.

□

2

Indian Nationalist Movement

The freedom movement of India continued for a long period. It began formally with the establishment of Congress in 1885, which continued with several ebbs and tides till 15 August 1947 without a break. India's national movement can be classified into three phases:

First Phase (from 1885 to 1905): Upto this time, it sufficiently nurtured but its objective was not clear. At that time, this movement was being represented by little educated intellectuals and middle-class people. This section of society was under the influence of Western moderate and extremist ideology.

Second Phase (from 1903 to 1919): Till this time, Indian National Congress had become quite mature and its aims and objectives were clear. Indian public initiated attempts to start social, economical, political and cultural development swing this platform. During this period, few aggressive extremist organisations opted for revolutionary pattern of West only to finish the British empiredom.

Third and Last Phase (from 1919 to 1947): During this period, Congress agitated to gain 'complete self-rule', i.e. Purna Swarajya under the leadership of Mahatma Gandhi.

The Factors Supporting Rise of Indian Nationalism

Year 1857 is considered as the beginning of the rise of nationalism following causes are attributed for this rise of: Western education and culture very significantly played a role in awakening nationalistic feelings and emotions. English had never got the Indians educated so as to awaken nationalism in them. Instead their aim was to fulfil the need of clerks-supply to British administration and commercial officers. But it was the misfortune of English people that Indians got to understand and ponder over ideas, opinions of Wirk, Mill, Gladstone, Bright, Macaulay, etc., the significant philosophers. They got an opportunity to read poetry of Milton, Shelley, Byron, etc., the great poets who themselves were struggling with barbaric policies of England as well as that of being familiar with philosophy of great philosophers like Voltaire, Rousseu, Mazzini. In this way, nationalistic emotions were germinated due to influence of Western education. English had made a medium to deliver education in 1833. Indians came to know about the then prevailing ill-customs in India. Owing to contact with Western countries, study of Western literature, science, history and philosophy and, along with it, nationalistic emotions were aroused in their heart.

Newspaper and press contributed significantly in the rise of nationalism.

Raja Ram Mohan Roy laid the foundation of national press. He edited papers like *Samvad Kaumudi* (Bangla) and *Mirat-ul-akhabar* (Persian) to initiate political awakening in India. In 1859, Ishwar Chandra Vidyasagar edited weekly paper *Sonprakash* anointed with nationalistic emotions. The grandfather of modern Khari Hindi, Bhartendu Harish Chandra had mentioned aggressive policy of Britishers toward India in his play *Bharat-Durdasha* in 1876. In this arena, creations of Pratap Narayan Mishra, Bal Krishna Bhatt, Badri Narayan Chaudhary besides Harish Chandra were imbued in patriotic emotions. Patriotic emotions and aspirations are also there in creations of other languages, for example, Mohammad Hussain and Altaf Hussain in Urdu literature, Bankim Chandra Chatterji in Bangla, Chiploonkar in

Marathi, Narmada in Gujarati, Subrahmanium Bharti in Tamil, etc.

Economic exploitation contributed greatly in awakening nationalism. Dada Bhai Nauorji drew a sketch of English exploitation, after grasping principle of 'wealth-expulsion'. English economic policy against India awakened repulsion against foreign rule and attachment to Swadeshi, i.e. indigenous goods and 'Swaraj', i.e. self-rule.

The extreme limits of economic exploitation of India can be witnessed during the reign of Lord Wilton.

There was a lack of political unification in India before arrival of English authorities. Indian borders were totally disrupted after reign of Mughal Emperor Aurangzeb. Political unification became possible due to the establishment of English empire.

Arrival/availability of fast transport and communication devices, like rail, post, telegraph, etc. strengthened nationalism in India.

Railways played a central role in all this. Edison Asnold has written – "Railways has provided that fulfilment which large and great countries never could have earlier which Akbar could not do with his kindness and Tipu with his aggression; they could not unify India into one country."

Intellectual reawakening played an important role in the rise of nationalism. Raja Ram Mohan Roy, Dayanand Saraswati, Swami Vivekanands, etc. agitated Indian sub-consciousness. In this context, Dayanand Saraswati said Swadeshi raj is the highest and the best of all. Swami Ramteerth said, "I am India personified, whole of India is my body."

Researches by few European intellectuals, like Sir William Johns, Monniere Williams, Max Mueller, Roth, Samson McDonald, etc. introduced us with ancient cultural heritage of India and certainly inferiority complex of Indian conscious disappeared. Self-respect and self-confidence were aroused in them to encourage their mind with emotions of patriotism and nationalism.

The discrimination against Indians in every field like army, industry, government services and economic sector also gave birth to nationalism.

The Situation Before Indian National Congress

During important efforts done before founding Indian National Congress, for the same Hume wrote a letter on 1 March, 1833, for graduates of Calcutta University in which he appealed to collectively attempt for independence. This appeal made a good impact on educated Indians. They started feeling the need of an All India Organisation. The very first step in this direction was certainly taken in September 1884 when annual session of Theosophical Society was held at Adyar (in erstwhile Madras, now Chennai). Dada Saheb Nauroji, Surendra Nath Bennerji, etc. joined in this session along with Hume. After this in 1884, an all-India organisation named, 'Indian National Union', was established. The main aim of establishing the organisation was to consult national social problems faced by the Indians. Meanwhile, Hume consulted the current Viceroy, Lord Dufferin and it is believed that, 'Indian National Congress' was the brainchild of Dufferin only. Dufferin also desired to gather Indian politicians once every year when they could express their real feelings towards the government through their suggestions to highlight administrative defects and its remedies so as to enable the administration stay cautious against future accidents. Hume agreed with Dufferin's plan. Hume, before establishing this organisation, visited England, where he consulted this issue in detail with politicians, like Rippon, Dalhousie, John Brights, Slag, etc. before returning to India. Hume founded an Indian parliamentary committee targeting generation of interest in members of British Parliament towards Indian problems. On return to India, Hume conducted a meeting of 'Indian National

Union' at Mumbai on 25 December 1885. Here name 'Indian National Union' was changed to 'Indian National Congress' or 'Bhartiya National Congress' after a discussion. Here only this institution was born. Earlier, its session was to be held at Pune but, owing to cholera epidemic breakout and spread there, the venue was shifted to Mumbai for organising the meeting.

Objectives of Indian National Congress

The objectives were to encourage mutual contact and friendship among Indians moving towards national welfare to nip the argument of religion, clan and states in the country, to encourage the emotion of national unity, discussing important and essential social issues with whole-hearted consent of educated class and deciding the direction and basic of efforts for Indian public's welfare in the years to come.

Proposals: The organisation presented its demands against the government through a nine suggestions in the meeting. These proposals were as follows:

1. To appoint an oath commission for inspecting Indian administrative legislature.
2. Expansion of State and Central legislature should be done.
3. Representatives should be elected instead of nominated members in the council.
4. Indian Civil Service exam should be conducted in both India and England and its maximum age-limit be increased from 19 years to 23 years.
5. Military expenditure should be cut-off.
6. Textiles imported from England should be retaxed for import duty.
7. Burma (now Myanmar), whose occupation was criticised, should be separated.
8. All the proposals should be sent to the political institutions of all the states so that the latter can demand execution of the same.

9. The next meeting of Congress should be held at Calcutta.

Various learned persons expressed their opinion upon foundation of Indian National Congress. Lala Lajpat Rai wrote in *Young India* that, "The main reason for establishing 'Indian National Congress', is that its founders were anxious to save the British empire from shattering." Biographer of Hume, Waderbesn wrote, "An object like a fearless security lamp is required to avoid increasing power of growing discontent in India and nothing better can be this security lamp than the Congress movement." Rajani Palm Dutt wrote in his book *India Today*, "Congress was founded in collusion with pre-decided secret plan of the British Government". Annie Besant wrote, "National Congress was originated by seventeen important Indians and Hume to defend motherland." Allen Octavian Hume, founder of Indian National Congress, was a citizen of Scotland. Hume worked on many important posts of Indian Civil Service for many years. He was appointed at the post of Chief Secretary of Indian National Congress. He wrote a heart-touching letter to the graduates of Calcutta University, before funding Indian National Congress, wherein he said:

"However wise and well-meaning scattered people may be, they are still powerless being alone. There is a need of union, organisation and a fixed clear-cut policy for execution. The yoke put on your shoulders will remain there till you would not be ready to labour accordingly, after accepting it as an absolute truth that self-sacrifice and selfless work only is the accurate guide to permanent bliss and freedom." In 1859, Hume cooperated to publish a newspaper called *Lok Mittra*. Hume refused the post of Lieutenant Governor from 1870 to 1879 because being on this post, he could not have served Indians in a true manner. He played an active role in the Congress for 22 years after 1885.

The First Phase of Movement (1885-1905)

In 1885, moderate national leaders established a sovereignty as soon as Indian moderate national leaders prevailing then were Dada Bhai Nauoji, Mahadev Govind Ranade, Feroze Shah Mehta, Surendra Nath Bannerji, Dinshaw Vacha, Vyomesh Chandra Bannerji, Gopal Krishna Gokhale, Madan Mohan Malviya, etc.

Congress policy was more than liberal during 20 years of Congress establishment. Therefore, this period is known as moderate or liberal national period in history of Congress. Founder members desired to develop absence of discrimination among religions and caste, equality in humans, equality before constitution, expanding civil-liberties and representative institutions. Moderate leaders considered only constitutional devices were capable of liberating our country.

In this period, prosperous once, middle-class intellectuals as advocates, doctors, engineers, journalists and litterateurs, assembled in the Congress, influenced it. Moderate leaders had full faith in justice of English people and these leaders considered Britishers not as their enemy but as friends. These leaders used to put their demands before the government through applications, representations, memorandum, reminders and delegation. During this period, Congress did not demand independence, instead asked for certain liberties. Among Congress demands were:

Expansion of legislative council, relaxation in age-limit for exam, simultaneous conduction of exams in India and England, enhanced recruitment, increased representation of Indians in the working committees of Viceroy and Governor, etc. These demands were framed in a very demeaning and inferior words as begging words in a legislative/legal manner. Owing to their this flexibility and controlled conduct, extremist leaders termed it as 'Political Beggarship'.

Popularity of Congress

Very gradually popularity of Congress enhanced. Earlier, this institution was represented by people of intellectual class but, after a time, it turned into institution of the general people. Owing to its popularity only, this institution acquired the size of the biggest political institution among the existing institutions.

Government's Point of View Towards Congress

In the initial years, government's point of view towards Congress was moderate but as the position of Congress kept on strengthening, it started to put its demands more emphatically before the government. This resulted in government's criticism of Congress after 1887. The attitude of government turned more hostile.

"Lord Dufferin, who contributed in founding Congress, criticising it, said its claim to represent Indian public appeared baseless. Congress represents such a negligible minority (not much negligible), vote which can never be handed over to the reins of a magnificent and multifarious empire." An English paper wrote its opinion of Congress as: "This is such a treasonful institution in a disguise, which has neither any representation of public and nor has it any values."

The British Government started instigating the Muslims with rebellion to isolate them from the Congress and they succeeded highly in their efforts when, in 1888, Sir Sayyed Ahmad Khan founded 'Anglo Muslim Defence Association' to resist the Congress being instigated by the British. In 1890, the Government servants were barred from joining Congress. Lord Curzon even went to the extent of saying, "Congress is staggering towards its downfall." One of the ambitions of Curzon was to aid Congress in its quiet death.

Gradually, the government policy towards Indians toughened instead of being liberal. Now it started to follow the policy of 'Divide and Rule'. Government could not succeed in oppression of Congress because this institution had large support of middle class. Dr. R.C. Majumdar has written – "Congress opposing British Governmental and bureaucratic campaigns could not succeed in their objective because they were unable to find out that Congress strength was based in middle class and not in rich donors group." Curzon termed Congress as 'dirty thing/piece, and taking treason (betrays)'.

Propaganda of Moderate in England

Leaders like Hume, Dada Bhai Nauroji had the opinion that Indian National Congress can be publicised much more from England than from India. In the year 1887, Nauroji established Indian Reform Society in London. In 1888, Dada Bhai Nauroji established 'Indian Association' under the Chairmanship of William Digvy. In 1889, Congress formed British Committee which started publication of a monthly magazine titled *India*. Through this medium, English people were made aware of the actual position in India. Congress sent its delegation to England time-to-time to eliminate and solve problems of the Indians. In 1890, the delegate visiting England consisted of Surendra Nath Bannerji, W.C. Bannerji and A.O. Hume as its members. In 1899, Vipin Chandra Pal visited England. As a consequence of all these efforts, a group with sympathetic attitude towards the problems of Indian public in mind was formed in England.

Many critics have bad-mouthed the achievements of moderate national leaders while extremists made fun of moderates', 'application and request' policy as 'Beggarship policy'. Lala Lajpat Rai wrote in this context: "They received stones instead of *rotis* (learned bread) after futile struggle of ending sorrows and having concessions for the last twenty years." There is no doubt that their present achievements were negligible and their many assumptions prove incorrect due to the changing nature of the nineteenth-century's British government. In whatever circumstances they took this difficult task in hand and difficulties they faced, considering those, their achievements cannot be neglected. They were successful in awakening emotions of national integration in subconscious of lower and middle-class. They introduced Indians to a common foe and through their very powerful economic reviews proved English to be the root cause of poverty, unemployment and economic backwardness.

If we deliver justice to progressive leaders like Dada Bhai Nauroji, Ferozeshah Mehta, Dinshaw Wacha, Gopal Krishna Gokhale, Surendra Nath Bannerji, then we will have to acknowledge that those were the most progressive elements and patriots of the prevailing Indian society. These people were responsible to get a 'Public Service Commission', appointed in 1886 and, in 1892, they got the legislature of Indian councils. The Government also appointed Welky Commission to evaluate and review the Indian expenditure on their insistence.

Partition of Bengal (1905)

At the time of partition, Bengal had the population of only seven crore and eighty-five lakh with today's Bihar, Odisha and Bangladesh included in Bengal. Bengal Presidency was the largest among the prevailing presidencies. In 1874, Assam got separated from Bengal. A Lieutenant Governor was unable to deliver efficient administration for such a large State. The then Governor-General Lord Curzon termed administrative inconvenience to be the main reason or the root cause of the Bengal Partition but the real cause was political and definitely not the administrative one.

At that time, Bengal was the central or focal point of the Indian national consciousness as well as the Bengalis possessed strong political awareness. To crush and trample this awareness, Lord Curzon wanted the partition of Bengal.

In December 1903, the news of Bengal partition spread all around. Many meetings were called as a mark of protest. Mostly these were at Dhaka, Memon Singh and Chatgaon. Bengal leaders like Surendra Nath Bannerji, Krishna Kumar Mittra, Prithvi Chandra Roy, etc. crticised the proposal of Bengal partition through newspapers like Bengal's *Hitwadi* and *Sanjeevani*. Even after protest, Lord Curzon declared Bengal partition. Resultantly, in Town Hall at Calcutta, a boycott proposal was passed on 7 August 1905. On 16 October 1905, partition became effective simultaneously with the declaration of Bengal partition. After partition, Bengal, Assam and few districts of East Bengal like Rajshahi, Dhaka and Chatgaon were annexed in East Bengal. The headquarter of this province was Dhaka. Inwest, Bengal included Bihar and Orissa along with West Bengal.

16 October 1905, the partition day was declared as 'Grievance Day' or 'Mourning Day' over the entire Bengal. News of Bengal partition fell on people like a bolt from the blue. Gopal Krishna had commented upon partition thus: "This was a cruel mistake." For the first time, fifty to seventy-five thousand people gathered in one single meeting to protest against Bengal partition. In protest against this partition, 'Swadeshi' and 'Boycott' movements were initiated. Banaras session of Congress also seconded 'Swadeshi' and 'Boycott' movements. Gradually, this movement started spreading all over the country. Tilak publicised this movement in Mumbai (erstwhile Bombay), Lala Lajpat Rai in Punjab and Uttar Pradesh, Syed Haider Raza in Delhi and Chidambaram Pillai in Madras (now Chennai).

Gopal Krishna also supported these 'Swadeshi' and 'Boycott' movements while chairing the Congress session at Banaras in 1905. Leaders of the extremist group, Tilak, Vipin Chandra Pal, Lajpat Rai and Arvind Ghosh wanted to spread this movement all over the nation. 'Swadeshi Bandhar Smiti', played an important role to gather public support at the time of Swadeshi Andolan. Ashwini Kumar Dutt founded this Samiti.

Dada Bhai Nauroji presented demand of 'Swarajya' or self-rule for the first time while chairing Congress session at Calcutta (now Kolkata) in 1906. Though the slogan 'Swarajya is my birthright', belongs to Bal Gangadhar Tilak, but credit for its maiden demand from the Congress platform goes to Dada Bhai Nauroji. After Bengal partition, the hold of aggressive leaders over national movement kept on tightening while moderate leaders opposed violence; the extremist leaders supported violence at the same time. In Calcutta session of Congress, the difference between ideology of both the sections was suppressed. In 1907, aggressive leaders of extremist ideology isolated themselves from Congress due to great divide between extremist and moderate leaders' opinions and due to opposite approach of running Swadeshi Movement. A huge public support was gathered against partition in-between Boycott and Swadeshi movements. Owing to this, the British Government had to cancel Bengal partition, at last in 1911 out of compulsion.

Second Phase of Movement (1905-1919)

During second phase of movement, on the one hand, revolutionary agitation and, on the other, extremist ones were carried on. Both these factions were struggling for the sole objective of liberation/release from extremist ideology of Britishers and for attaining complete 'self-rule', i.e., 'Poorna Swarajya'. At one side, extremist faction was struggling on the basis of Boycott movement, while at another side, aggressive revolutionary faction wanted to attain freedom using bombs and guns. While extremists believed in peaceful but active political movements, at the same time, revolutionaries believed in using force and violence to make Britisher run straight immediately out of India.

Causes of Rise of Extremism

Owing to scornful policy of British Government towards Congress demands, the younger leaders like Bal Gangadhar Tilak, Lala Lajpat Rai and Vipin Chandra Pal were agitated to the core of their heart. These young leaders never expressed faith in political begging of moderate or liberal leaders. They emphasized to the need for strong steps to make the government accept their demands.

Uprise of Hindu religion also contributed greatly in the rise of aggressive ideology. Liberal leaders of Congress expressed their full faith in Western civilisation and culture. On the other side, people like Swami Vivekanand, Dayanand Saraswati, Lala Lajpat Rai, Arvind Ghosh and Vipin Chandra Pal who proved their own civilisation and culture to be superior than Western culture, were also there. Arvind Ghosh declared: "Freedom is the aim of our life and Hindu religion alone will fulfil this aim. Nationality is a religion and it is a God's gift." Annie Besant concluded: "The entire Hindu system is much above the Western civilisation."

In the duration of 1876 to 1900, India had already fallen in the grip of famine for eighteen times, which caused big economic and public loss. One lakh and seventy-three thousand people were killed in the grip of plague at Bombay in 1897-98. Government did not make any such attempt so as to check the epidemic, instead maltreated their daughters and daughters-in-law at the pretext of checking plague. Tilak criticised this 'Black Deed' of the government harshly in his journal *Kesari*. As a consequence, he had to stay in prison for eighteen months. Chapekar brothers of Pune shot plague officers Rand and Amherst after getting frustrated of the excesses committed during plague. These incidents encouraged aggressive nationalism.

The quote of Lord Beacon that, "Excess of poverty and economic discontent give birth to revolution," is literally true in the context of India as object economic exploitation policy of Britishers actually gave birth to aggressive policy in India. Governmental policy keeping educated Indians away from employment also encouraged extremism. Dada Bhai Nauroji, exponent of 'Drain Theory', exposed Britishers' exploitative policies.

Contemporary international happenings also had contributed significantly in encouraging aggressive elements. Successful freedom struggles at Egypt, Persia and Turkey also encouraged and inspired Indians a lot. A backward and small nation like Ethiopia defeated a country like Italy in 1896. Then aggressive nationalist factions were actually encouraged by Japan's victory over Russia in 1905. Garret was of the opinion – "Defeat of Italy in 1897 provided great impulse and boost of force to Tilak's agitation."

Curzon's repercussive policies had a very strong backlash on Indian youths' conscious. The seven years' reign of Lord Curzon is called 'Period of delegations, commissions and commissioners'. The repercussive actions ordered by Lord Curzon, for example, Calcutta corporation legislature, university legislature and Bengal partition contributed significantly to encourage aggressive ideology.

Bal Gangadhar Tilak, Lala Lajpat Rai and Vipin Chandra Pal played a significant role in the revival of aggressive nationalism in India. This movement flourished under the able leadership of these leaders only. Tilak believed: "An inferior Swadeshi government is superior to a good foreign government and self-rule, i.e., Swarajya is my birthright, I will acquire this right in each and every situation."

Tilak made efforts for propagating nationalistic awareness among Indians by initiating 'Ganpati Utsav' and 'Shivaji Utsav'.

Lala Lajpat Rai said, "English people hate beggars quite much and I think beggars are also liable for hate. So, it is our duty to prove that we are not beggars." Vipin Chandra Pal led Bengal youths. He was considered as 'Army Chief of Tilak in Bengal'. Few other important reasons, like maltreatment meted out to Indians in colonies, social slur and in uncivil behaviour towards Indians were responsible to encourage aggressive nationalism in India.

Refusing the policy of 'Apply and Request', of moderates to get their demands accepted, extremists proclaimed it as 'political beggary'. Tilak declared, "Our aim is self-dependence and not beggarship." Vipin Chandra Pal said, "If the government asks me to have Swarajya, then I will only thank it for this gift and say I will not accept anything for which I have no capability to acquire the same." These leaders emphasized boycott of foreign goods, importance of national education and Satyagraha (persistence for truth) through acceptance of 'swadeshi' (use of indigenous things only). Liberal leaders wanted to contain 'Swadeshi' and 'Boycott' movements in Bengal only. Their Boycott movement was limited to 'Boycott' of foreign goods only but aggressive leaders desired to expand these movements in bigger area of country and to compare their Boycott movement with Mahatma Gandhi's non-cooperation movement. These desired to carry Boycott movement upto Non-cooperation movement and peaceful protest, 'Boycott' of not only foreign cloths, instead boycott of government schools, courts, titles, governmental services, etc.

Lala Lajpat Rai commented in the context of boycott, "We have directed ourselves away of Raj Niwas to hutments of penniless. This alone is the intended policy and spiritual importance of boycott movement."

Aggessive leaders advocated Indian welfare embedded in national education only and accepted this fact by heart. Vipin Chandra Pal said, "National education is the education that is conducted or imparted on the basis of national draft, controlled by representatives of country and is controlled and imparted in a manner which aims attainment of national destiny." Sir Surendra Nath Bannerji founded 'Rashtriya Shiksha Parishad', i.e. 'National Education Board' and Tilak founded 'Deccan Education Society'. Tilak advocated non-cooperation with the government.

Revolutionary and Aggressive Agitation

Persons with revolutionary ideology having faith in politics of bombs and pistols used not to have even an iota of faith in politics of treaty or compromise. Their objective was 'Give life or take life'. Bomb politics became essential for them because they could not find a way to express their emotions or struggle for the freedom. Aggressive sect wanted a very quick result. They never believed in liberals 'inspiration and extremists' slow-effect policy. They considered murdering, committing robberies, dacoity, robbing banks, post offices and trains, etc., all the actions are totally legal. Majority of supporters of revolutionary ideology were mostly in Bengal. They used to have an aversion towards British rule. They wanted to shoo away Britishers instantly with their bags and baggage. After 'Warisan Conference' on 22 April 1906, newspaper *Yugantar* wrote: "The solution is with people themselves. Thirty crore people living in India, will have to raise their sixty crores hands to stop this and curse of exploitation. Excess should be checked with excess only (i.e. a thorn can be removed using a thorn only or policy of 'tit for tat'). These revolutionary young men adopted ways of Irish terrorists and Russian 'Nihilists'." During this period, many terrorist strikes were preformed in many parts of the country, mainly Bengal, Maharashtra and Punjab.

If it is said that Bengal was the fort of revolutionary movement, then it will be no hyperbola. Barindra Kumar Ghosh and Bhupendra Dutt (Vivekanand's brother) propagated revolutionary ideology in Bengal. In 1906, both the young men together published a newspaper called *Yugantar*. Revolutionary movement was started by 'Bhadralok Samaj' or Gentlemen's Society. This newspaper contributed maximum in instilling revolution all over the country. Political and religious education was propagated among common public. The 'Anusheelan Samiti' was formed at Midnapur in 1907 with the cooperation of Barindra Ghosh and Bhupendra Dutt only. Its objective was 'Blood for Blood'. Apart from 'Anusheelan Samiti' and 'Sahsidaya Samiti', 'Swadeshi Bandav Samiti', 'Prati Samiti', etc. conducted revolutionary activities. Many revolutionary ideology-inspired newspapers were also started being published from Bengal only. Out of these *Sandhya Vandematram Yugantar* were prominent ones. *Yugantar* expressed its reaction to police *lathicharge* in *Parimal* (the Journal) – "Thirty crores of population should raise its sixty crore hands to stop the oppression undertaken by the British government. Let the force be faced with force only."

Name of Hemchandra Kanungo is specially mentionable among the Bengal revolutionaries. At Paris, he received military training from a Russian. He opened a bomb-manufacturing workshop/makeshift factory in 'Maniktalla' area of Calcutta in 1908 after his return to India.

On 23 December 1907, ex-District Magistrate of Dhaka, Allen was shot in the back. Prafulla Chaki and Khudi Ram Bose threw bomb on Kingsford to kill him but he escaped from it. Chaki shot himself to get rid of police trap while Khudi Ram Bose was caught. In the end, Bose was hanged on 11 May 1908. After this incident, police raided Maniktalla and 34 accused were arrested, including Barindra Kumar Ghosh and Arvind Ghosh. A case under 'Alipur Conspiracy' was filed, charged and run over all these. Barindra Ghosh was delivered life sentence and Arvind Ghosh was acquitted in lack of suitable evidences.

One more revolutionary from Bengal was Jatin Nath Mukherjee, who was titled and known by the name of 'Bagha Jatin'. He was killed in a police encounter at Balasore on 9 September 1915. Ras Behari Bose was one of the great revolutionaries, who throw bombs upon Lord Hardinge during shifting of capital from Calcutta to Delhi. Ras Behari Bose went away to Japan to escape arrest. Awadh Behari, Amir Chandra, Bal Mukund and Vasant Kumar were arrested and a case was registered against them under Delhi conspiracy.

To suppress revolutionary activities going on in Bengal, the government tried to uproot terrorism using support of explosive material legislative in 1900 and newspaper legislature of 1908. Owing to continued oppression of British Government, Arvind Ghosh turned ascetic, i.e. Sannyasi, renouncing revolutionary activities and established an Ashram or hermitage in Pondicherry. Brahma Bandopadhyay, who addressed Ravindra Nath Thakur as 'Gurudev' for the first time, became a Swamiji at Ram Krishna Math.

In 1906, a revolutionary movement spread through Punjab all over due to 'Upniveshikaran Vidheyak', i.e. 'Colonisation Act' of Punjab Government. Its aim was to discourage land holding consolidations and to intervene in rights of 'property partition'. Meanwhile, government decided to increase 'water tax'. Therefore great discontent spread among public. Looking at this typhoon, the government got anxious. It banned public meetings with at the point of view of crushing the agitation. At Rawalpindi, it arrested Lala Lajpat Rai and Ajit Singh to send them to Mandley prison. In 1915, draft of an organised movement was prepared in Punjab, in which it was decided to sound bugle of revolution in the entire north India simultaneously, on the same date of 21 February 1915. The government got an inkling of this plan. Many leaders were arrested and they were punished in Lahore conspiracy case. Prithvi Singh, Parmanand, Kartar Singh, Vinayak Savarkar, Jagat Singh, etc. were among them. After establishing 'Gadar Party' in America, Punjab became prominent centre for activities of this party. Ajit Singh had founded an institution called 'Anjuman-e-Mohiwane-Vatan' and had Published the newspaper called *Bharatmata*.

Credit goes to Tilak's paper *Kesari* to throw light on the revolutionary movement in Maharashtra. Tilak started celebrating 'Shivaji Utsav' in 1893. Its objective was more of a political nature than the religious one. Plague spread in Maharashtra during 1893-97 and the British government enhanced its oppressive activities instead of applying balm to it (i.e. to pacify). At last, on 22 June 1897, Commissioner for Plague Eradication, Amherst was shot dead. In this connection, Kamodar Chapekar was caught and hanged to death. In 1908, the government let all the hell loose on four of the vernacular newspapers. Tilak was re-arrested on 24 June 1908 and, on the basis of the articles published in *Kesari*, first a case was registered on him; then he was sentened for six years imprisonment. The workers strongly agitated to protest against it at Bombay and it continued for six days. Nasik was also one of the forts of revolutionary agitation in Maharashtra. Vinayak Damodar Savarkar founded an association called 'Mittra Mela' at Nasik in 1904.

This mela or fair changed to 'Abhinav Bharat' after pattern of magazine's young Italy. The main member of this association, Anant Lakshman Karkare shot to kill Justice Jackson. A case was registered over the persons connected with this murder case under the name of 'Nasik conspiracy case'. This resulted in the declaration of life-sentence punishment to Sawarkar's brother Ganesh. The important revolutionary journal *Kal* was edited in Maharashtra.

Revolutionary Movement on Foreign Soil

Revolutionaries continued freedom struggle of India from foreign shores of escape grip of British Rule. During first phase of revolutionary movement only, in 1915, Raja Mahendra Pratap founded interim Indian government in Kabul with the help of Germany. Other cooperative members of the cabinet consisted of Maulana Abdulla, Maulana Bashir, C. Pillai, Sham Sher Singh, Dr. Mathura Singh, Khuda Baksh, Mohammad Ali as prominent ones. During this period, Raja Mahendra Pratap met Lenin for gathering the support to his government. In February 1905, Shyamji Krishna Verma established 'Indian Home Rule Society', in London from out of India. It is termed as 'India House'. This society published a journal called *Indian Sociologist*. Soon 'India House' became the focus of the movement for the Indians residing in London. Other members of this association were Hardayal, Madan Lal Dhingra, Vinayak Damodar Sawarkar, etc. Madan Lal Dhingra shot dead the political leader to Indian secretary William Hut Curzon Boyli on 1 July 1909. Dhingra was arrested to be hanged till death. After this muder incident, Savarkar was arrested and sent to India to face legal action under 'Nasik conspiracy case'. Another colleague of Shyamji Krishna Verma was Madame Bhikaji Cama. She belonged to a Parsi family of Maharashtra. In 1902, she left India and canvassed against the British regime in India across different European countries. She participated in the 'International Socialist Congress', on behalf of the Indian side at Stuatgart (Germany) in 1907. She unfurled the Indian tricoloured flag here only. Madame Cama is called 'Mother of Indian Revolution'. In 1908, India House decided to celebrate golden jubilee of the great revolution of 1857.

Savarkar named this rebellion as Indian Freedom Struggle.

In 1913, many Indian people established 'Gadar Party' at San Francisco (America) under the leadership of Lala Hardayal Singh. Sohan Singh was the president of this party, and Lala Hardayal Singh was the secretary of publicity department. This organisation established Yugantar Press and started publishing a weekly paper called *Gadar* from 1 November 1913.

In World War I, owing to confrontation of Germany and Britain, the former established an Indian Independence Committee to aid the Indian revolutionaries financially as well as helped in the supply of arms and ammunition.

Congress Session at Calcutta (1906): Test of Power

There was enough rift among the opinions of moderates and extremists at Calcutta Congress Session of 1906. While the extremists wanted to select Bal Gangadhar Tilak as the Congress president, moderates kept on protesting the move. In these circumstances, moderates or liberals called back Dada Bhai Nauroji from England and appointed him president of the Congress session at Calcutta. Efficient leadership of Dada Bhai Nauroji saved Congress from this potential fissure. Differences of opinions were not finished but at least subsided effectively to reflect its impression in the Congress session. At Surat, extremists were successful to get four proposals passed, namely securing home rule; adopting national education; encouragement of Swadeshi or indigenous movement and boycott of foreign cloth. Dada Bhai Nauroji first of all presented the demand of 'Swarajya' or 'self-rule/home rule' in the Congress session at Calcutta.

Congress Session at Surat (1907): Split in Congress

Surat Session of Congress in 1907 became extremely important from the historical point of view. The session was held at the banks of river Tapti on 26 December 1907. Moderate and extremist factions had a great wide in their opinions regarding Home Rule Movement (Swaraj) pattern and election for the post of the president of the session. Extremists wanted to appoint Tilak as the first preference and then Lala Lajpat Rai as the second one. But moderates appointed Dr. Ras Behari Bose as the president of this session. Even before the commencement of the elections, an ugly fight broke between two factions' leaders so as to split the Congress into sections. Annie Besant commented: "Surat incident is the most sorrowful incident in the history of Congress." After partition at Surat, Lala Lajpat Rai and Vipin Chandra Pal led the Extremists group and Gopal Krishna Gokhale became the leader of Moderate group. In 1916, at Lucknow session of Congress, both the groups again merged mutually.

Founding the Muslim League (1906)

Under the leadership of H.H. Agha Khan, a group of Muslims met Viceroy Lord Minto on 1 October 1906 at Shimla. The perpetuator of this representative delegation was Earthboule, the principal of Aligarh College. This delegation requested Viceroy to establish a separate communal selection system for the Muslims. Visit of this Muslim delegation was badly handled by the English authorities. Minto supported their demands completely and consequently the Muslim leaders founded the Muslim League under the leadership of Nawab of Dhaka on 30 December 1906. Nawab Sakim-Ul-Allah-Khan was the founder president of the Muslim League while the very first session was chaired by Mushtaq Hussain. The main aim of this Association was to generate a feeling of dedication in the hearts of the Indian Muslims towards the British government and to defend political rights and other ones of the Indian Muslims. The Muslim League demanded separate election zones for the Muslims, which were granted in 1909 through Morley-Minto Reforms. The League never demanded political rights of Indians except supporting Indian National Congress on the basis of Lucknow Pact of 1916.

Morley-Minto Reforms (1909)

When Lord Minto became the Governor of India, the whole of India was gradually moving towards political unrest. Lord Minto himself wrote about this political unrest: "The duststorm of Indian political unrest was hidden under seemingly quiet surface and most of it was entirely justifiable."

Indian Secretary Morley and Viceroy Lord Minto passed Indian Council Act, 1909 for reforms, which were named as 'Morley-Minto Reforms'. The act was passed on 25 May 1909 and on 15 November 1909, it became functional after legal censure. Size and authorities of central and provincial councils were enhanced under this Act. But even now, majority of representatives were to be elected indirectly. There was even a provision of appointing one Indian member in the executive council of Governor-General. Members were authorised to put proposal and raise questions under this Act. Right to vote for budget proposals was also there for them. Even after all this, councils had no actual rights in practice. The primary object of Morley-Minto Reforms was to divide nationalistic camp and to break the Indian unity by encouraging Muslim communisation. Separate electoral zones and right to vote were arranged for Muslims. After this very policy of Britishers turned to be the root cause of partition of India. Congress protested these reforms/ amendments while staunch Muslims supported them. Viceroy Minto had written: "Remember that we are sowing such a fatal poison-seed through separate electoral zones, whose harvest will be more than bitter."

Treason Assembly Act (1911)

The extremist organisations enhanced their rebellious activities very fast as a reaction to Morley-Minto amendments. Consequently, the British government passed Treason Assembly Act in 1911 to attempt nipping the movement through the arrest of extremist leaders like Lala Lajpat Rai and Ajit Singh.

Delhi Court (1911)

In 1911, a grand Darbar (court) was organised to welcome Emperor George V and Empress Mary of England. At that time, Lord Hardinge was the Viceroy of India. Bengal Partition was declared 'null' in this court and alongside a separate province uniting all the Bengali-speaking zones. Orissa and Bihar also became the states on the basis of a new declaration. The shifting of capital of India from Calcutta of Delhi was declared in this very court, though actual legal transfer of capital to Delhi could be materialised only in 1912.

Kama-Gata-Maru Episode/Scandal

Owing to 1914, Kama-Gata-Maru scandal, Canadian government banned entry of those Indians who were directly arriving from India. In those days, transportation was not so developed so as to enable one travel so far without any stoppage or halt using the same boat. But in 1913, Canadian Supreme Court sanctioned rights of entry to 35 Indians, who did not arrive directly from India. Encouraged by this decision/ruling, India's Gurdeep Singh hired a ship called 'Kama-Gata-Maru' and left for Canada's port, Vancouver with 376 other passengers. On arriving at the seashore, Indians were escorted and banned from entering the country by Canadian police. Hussain Rahim, Sohan Lal Pathak and Balwant Singh formed a 'Shore Committee' to contest case of these travellers. The Canadian government expelled this ship out of their country's borders. Even before this ship could reach 'Yokoholma', the WW-I broke out. The British government in India ordered to bring back this ship directly to Calcutta. On arrival of the ship, many hiccups and altercations took place between the passengers and police in Calcutta. These ambushes killed eighteen passengers and two hundred and two of these were put into prison.

Lucknow Session of Congress (1916)

The Congress partition at Surat Session (1907) continued till 1916. Meanwhile, on one hand, the government kept on oppressing terrorist activities, while the other hand, rift between Hindu and Muslim opinions was deepening. Moderate leaders, Gopal Krishna Gokhale and Feroze Shah Mehta died in the year 1915. Bal Gangadhar Tilak and Annie Besant took up efforts to gather extremists and moderates, both of these under one roof of the Congress platform. Their efforts were even rewarded. In 1916 Ambica Charan Majumdar chaired the Lucknow Congress Session.

Indian Muslims were annoyed with the English Government after Balcan war. At that time, Maulana Abul Kalam Azad, Shankar Ali, Mohammad Ali Jinnah, etc., prominent leaders of the Muslim League passed proposal of 'Swarajya Prapti' or 'Attainment of Home Rule' in Lucknow session. In 1916, a pact was signed between Muslim League leader Mohammad Ali Jinnah and Congress, owing to which Congress and League shook hands to establish a combined committee. Under the provision of the pact, Congress accepted demand of community-based representation of the Muslim League. Later, its consequences were fierce and fatal. This pact is also known as 'Lucknow Pact'. Many senior leaders like Madan Mohan Malviya were totally against this pact. They blamed this pact to be tilted towards interest of Muslim League.

Home Rule League Movement

Home Rule movement, that aimed to acquire home rule through legal means under the British empire, had prominent leaders as Bal Gangadhar Tilak and Mrs. Annie Besant. Tilak established 'Home Rule League' for obtaining home rule on 28 April 1916 in Belgaon. The league established by him was effective up to Karnataka, Maharashtra and Central Province. Tilak established six branches of the league, one each in Central Maharashtra, Mumbai (erstwhile Bombay), Karnataka and Central Province and two in Barar. He enhanced his publicity campaign by publishing six Marathi and two English journals. He said, making public understand the need of home rule, that "India is like the son who is grown young now. It is the demand of time that a guardian or father should confer on him his proper rights." Tilak linked demands of education in regional languages and states on the basis of language with demand of Swarajya. Tilak celebrated the first anniversary of their League at Nasik in May 1917. After her return to India, Annie Besant started publishing a weekly paper *Common Week* from 2 January 1914 and a daily paper *New India* from 14 July 1914. Annie Besant awakened the desire of liberation and political will among the Indians. She established 'Home Rule League' in September 1916 at Madras (now Chennai) through the example of Ireland and appointed George Arrow Dale as its secretary. V.P. Wada and C.R. Ramaswamy Aiyyer were included as the colleagues of Mrs. Annie Besant. Leaders like Jawaharlal Nehru, V. Chakravarty, J. Bannerji, etc. also accepted the membership of the league. Members of Servants of India Society established by Gopal Krishna Gokhale were not allowed to join the league. The onus to increase influence of league in all the regions, without the boundary of influence any of Tilak Home Rule League, fell on Annie Besant. The maximum number of offices of 'Home Rule League' were located at Madras.

Later, the British Government arrested Annie Besant and her two colleagues in 1917 owing to the risk of fear by the rising influence of the league. S. Subramanium Aiyyer returned the title of his 'Knighthood' in protest of this arrest. Tilak wanted to go on Satyagraha to protest the arrest and the British Government released Annie Besant. She became the president of the Calcutta session of Congress in 1917. She was the first lady to become the Congress president. As its president, she expressed: "Now India is standing on her own two legs to acquire its right and not on its knees to take its favours." Feeling pressure from all around India, Secretary Montagu passed a proposal in the British Parliament on 20 August 1917. This proposal had words aimed towards handing over India, a responsible and answerable rule. As a result, Annie Besant declared the suspension of 'Home Rule League' itself on 20 August 1917.

Declaration of 20 August 1917

The British Prime Minister Lyod George appointed Edwin Montague as the India Secretary with a view to console the Indian public. Montague was considered a supporter of the Indian nationalistic ideas. Montague declared in the British Parliament: "Demand of educating Indians is certainly their right and they must be confessed this right to hold responsibility and of self-decision."

The Indian Secretary Montague read a proposal in House of Commons at Britain on 20 August 1917, that advocated for increased rights of Indians' representation in every department of the Indian administration. This was called 'Montague Declaration'. Moderates termed Montagu's declaration as 'Magna Carta of India'. Montague arrived India in November 1917. Here after exhaustive consultations and discussions with the current Viceroy Lord Chelmsford, issued 'Montague-Chelmsford Report in the year 1919. India Government Act, 1919 was formed on the basis of this 'Montague Declaration' and 'Montague-Chelmsford Report' was termed as a link between the government formed by Montague Parliament and Indian public's representatives. Dual administration was arranged through this Act called 'India Government Act, 1919'.

Lokmanya Tilak pronounced this act as unsatisfactory, disappointing and a morning bereaved of sun. In the year 1919, Congress in its Amritsar session opinionated these reforms as insufficient and disappointing. Congress was again cleared into half owing to reforms of the year 1919. Moderate leaders under the leadership of Surendra Nath Bannerji welcomed Montague reforms in the year 1918 and founded an All India Liberal Association after getting separated from Congress.

The legislative reforms of the year 1919 were regulated in 1921. Under this Act, provincial matters were divided for the first time into reserved and conferred categories. Also, for the first time, Indian Legislative Council received rights to present budget and also the first-time provision for establishing Public Service Commission was made. There was a provision to appoint a legislative commission for reviewing the 1919 Act. Ten years later this commission was known as, 'Simon Commission'.

Rowlett Act (1919)

The British Government appointed a committee under the chairmanship of Sir Sydney Rowlett to curb the influence of the revolutionaries and to oppress idea of nationalism in India. The committee presented its report in 1918. Two legislatures were included in the central legislative council in February 1919 on the basis of suggestions handed over by the committee's efforts. The sanction of these acts are is known as 'Rowlett Act' or 'Black Act'. This Act was regulated on 8 March 1919 even after stiff protest by the Indian leaders. This Act had an arrangement that sanctioned the magistrates the authority to arrest and register a case on any suspicious person; also that the person could be kept in jail for an indefinite period. In this way, with this right, the government could punish and present any innocent person the way it wished. In this manner, suspension of the law related to present a prisoner in person to the court, i.e. habeas-corpus, which was the foundation of civil liberties in Britain, was obtained by the government through Rowlett Act. This Act was also termed as 'Law without appeal, without pleader, without plea'. This is also known as 'Black Act' and 'Terrorist Crime Act'. By now, Gandhiji had appeared in the Indian politics. On 6 April 1919, he conducted a nationwide strike to protest this Act. Swami Shraddhanand had the reins of this movement in Delhi, where five of the agitators were injured in firing over the crowds. Crowds were also fired at in Punjab and Lahore. Mahatma Gandhi left for Delhi after accepting invitation from Swami Shraddhanand and Dr. Satpal. Gandhi established 'Satyagrah Sabha' against the Rowlett Act by criticising the same. The other members of the society were Lal Das, Dwarka Das, Shankarlal Banker, Omar Somani , V.G. Harneyman, etc. They were arrested on the way in Palwal (Haryana) on 8 April 1919 and were sent to Mumbai, from where they reached Ahmedabad on 13 April 1919. Till that moment, the situation had become quite normal.

Jallianwala Bagh Massacre (13 April 1919)

Due to ban on entry of Gandhiji and few other leaders in Punjab, the public there was quite agitated. This frustration enhanced further, when two popular leaders of Punjab, Dr. Satpal and Dr. Saif-ud-din Kichlu were arrested without any reason and logic by the Amritsar Deputy Commissioner. Public took out a peaceful procession to protest against this arrest. Police prohibited this procession from moving ahead and fired on the marching crowd after failing to contain the procession. Consequentially, two of the persons were killed. The procession turned violent. The government buildings were put on fire and five English men were murdered. The government handed over the city administration to the military officers, namely Brigadier General R. Dyer on 10 April 1919 after being unsettled by the situation of the Amritsar city. On 12 April 1919 Dyer got few persons arrested. On 13 April 1919, i.e. Baisakhi day, around four o'clock in the evening, a meeting was called in Jalliawala Bagh, gathering twenty thousand people. On the other hand, Dyer declared the meeting illegal or non-constitutional at 9.30 am the same day. Intense lecturing was going on for the release of Dr. Satpal and Dr. Kichlu along with the protest against Rowlett Act. In this vulnerable situation, Dyer ordered the crowd to disperse within three minutes. Then he took position at the garden's main entrance gate. Around 1,650 shots of 303 rifles were fired, which killed one thousand people and injured three times more, i.e. 3,000. However, the government reported 379 casualties and 1,200 injured. In this massacre, an Indian named Hansraj aided Dyer. Deenbandhu F. Andrews termed this massacre as intentionally committed cruel murders. Even Montague bitterly criticised this genocide as, 'eradication murders'. At the time of Jalianwala Bagh massacre, Michael O'Dyer was the Lieutenant Governor of Punjab. He commented in the context of R. Dyer's action that the action was alright and Governor had accepted it.

After this barbaric massacre, on 15 April 1919, martial law was imposed in Punjab, Gujranwala, Kasoos Shekupura and Wazirabad, when around 298 persons were arrested and punished in different ways. Gopal Krishna Gokhale resigned from the Viceroy's executive committee to protest against this massacre. Frustrated and grieved, Ravindranath Tagore surrendered his title 'Sir'. He also said, "The time has arrived when medals of honour make blotch on us obvious in the illogical context of dishonour. Where I am concerned, I want to stand with my countrymen devoid of all special titles." Garret had written about this accident: "Amritsar massacre was an era turning tragic mishappening at par to 1857 revolt for relation between India and Britain."

On 1 October 1919, in utter helplessness, the government appointed a Commission on Jalianwala Bagh Tragedy. There were five British and three Indians among this eight-membered commission. The Indian National Congress appointed a commission of its own under the guidance of Madan Mohan Malviya to examine this merciless occurrence. Hunter Committee presented its report on March 1920. Just prior to it, the government had got an 'Indemnity Bill' passed to save/defend the culprit responsible. The commission tried to whitewash the entire episode. The Punjab Governor was declared 'not guilty'. The Committee harassed Dyer a little and said that "Dyer used excessive force to fulfil his duty but he did it with devotion whatever he had to do."

The Indian Secretary Montague said, "General Dyer acted accordingly what he perceived correct and he acted with absolute pure intentions, although he committed a mistake in analysing the situation." Dyer was punished for his crime through termination of his services. The British newspapers hailed Dyer as 'Protector of British Empire' and British House of Lords called him 'Lion of British Empire'. The British government conferred on him the title of 'Sword of Honour' for his services. The examination committee appointed by the Congress targeted the authorities as 'condemnable' for this barbaric act. The Congress also emphasized demand to take action against the culprits and deliver financial aid to the killed ones' families. But the government did not pay any heed at all to this issue. Therefore, Gandhiji broke ground of build up of 'Non-cooperation movement'. At the time of Jalianwala Bagh massacre, only a 'Danda Fauz' or 'Staff Army' was constructed under the leadership of Chamandeep in Punjab. Its members braced with latish and bird-killing guns, i.e. airguns, took rounds on the roads and pasted posters.

The Third Phase of Movement (1919-1947): Gandhi Era

Gandhiji was one among the shining stars of national integration. Gandhiji returned to India after the completion of studies of barristership from England. From here, he went to Africa in the year 1893 and there he kept on struggling against colour discriminatory policy of the British government, all through his twenty years' long stay there. Gandhiji started 'Satyagraha movement' here only for the first time. In January 1915, Gandhiji arrived India and came in contact with Gopal Krishna Gokhale, whom he accepted as his political 'Guru'. Gandhiji attached himself with active Indian politics under the influence of Gokhale only.

The British government was entrapped in WW-I at the moment Gandhiji entered Indian politics. Gandhiji co-operated with the government completely due to his belief that the British government will itself gift the Indians 'Swarajya' as a return gesture of their cooperation after the war got over. Gandhiji encouraged people to join the army. Consequently, some people started calling him 'Recruiting Sergeant' also.

In 1916, Gandhiji established 'Sabarmati Ashram' near Ahmedabad and, in April 1917, he started agitation against exploitation and torture of farmers at district Champaran situated in Bihar. Here the European Indigo planters (plantation owners) were committing excess maltreatment against farmers working in the Indigo plantation.

A large number of farmers at Champaran invited Gandhiji after coming to know of his success stories in

South Africa. The workers had to cultivate at least one-and-a-half times of their land. Also they had to compulsively sell their harvest at the price fixed by the European Indigo planters. Under similar conditions, Bengal farmers had got riddance from the European Bengal owners (planters) in 1859-1860. In 1917, Gandhiji arrived at Champaran with Dr. Rajendra Prasad, Mazhar-ul-Haque, J.P. Kripalani, Narhari Parikh and Mahadev Desai, and started inspecting/examining the circumstances of farmers. The government had to form an 'Inspection Committee', out of compulsion. Gandhiji himself was its member. His effort lessened the problems of farmers. In 1918, Gandhiji organised 'Non-tax Movement', at Khera district of Gujarat. The same year, Gandhiji intervened the debacle between Ahmedabad workers and mill owners to increase their wages by 35%. In the initial days of his politics, Gandhiji appreciated the Legislative amendment process of the British government but post-Jaliawala Bagh massacre of 1919, Gandhiji's entire point of view related to the government had been overhandled.

□

3

Background

The time period of Indian history, when the birth of Gopal Krishna Gokhale took place, deeply influenced his life and his future life also changed accordingly. He was born nine years after the 1857 revolt. For the first time, Indians had challenged the British rule in 1857 only. In the 1885, when Indian National Congress was born with an aim of securing India's independence through constitutionally approved actions, Gopal Krishna was quite young at the moment. Gopal Krishna had expired five years before Mahatma Gandhi initiated the non-violence movement for the first time in India. Gandhiji considered him as his political 'Guru'.

In 1858, the East India Company's rule over India ended and the reign of Queen Victoria started. New changes and modifications, and new assumptions, new ideas were required in political, social, economic and educational fields under new administrative process.

New ideas were emerging in the country. This time period was full of challenges for the intellectuals and learned persons of the country. They were apprehensive of hanger as Indian tradition, culture, history, social system, religion and rituals and customs. Poverty of people kept on increasing as well as they were compelled to bear stings of slavery. At that time the people had a query how to regain lost honour of the Indians.

The English rulers had their own pleas to support slavery of India. They always kept on repeating that Indians are the victims of backwardness due to their own social ill-customs, caste discrimination, female exploitation and other negative characters.

This argument of Britishers was but only partially true. Indian thinkers had not accepted English logic related to freedom-curbing and loss. Thinkers' point of view was changing extensively. The thinkers/philosophers had paid special attention to reforms in social structure, before establishing the Indian National Congress. Before the rise of the Indian National Congress, Associations such as Bombay Presidency Association, Calcutta Association, Annie's 'Sarvajanik Sabha', Madras Mahajan Sabha were already active in political arena but these emphasized the aim of social reforms. They believed in highlighting the way to political liberty through social reforms only. On the other hand, there was also a class which wanted to keep social change and politics separate. A very sharp cleavage of opinions between supporters of both types of ideology was apparent.

A very prominent section was also present in the country that considered downfall in moral and spiritual life of public as the root cause of the country's political fall. Swami Vivekanand and other personalities canvassed the message of Hindu religion at large. Many Associations also started their efforts to propagate spirituality among countrymen. Few associations became active in foreign countries as well and a desirable change to the image of Indians started appearing in the foreigners' mindset. An assumption kept on strengthening among the public that no change in situation is possible without applying opting media of sacrifice or struggle, patriotism, spirituality, sacrifice and struggle.

The East India Company never considered it essential to think over India's future till its rule would continue here. When the British rule was initiated, then obviously a hope for rule of law in the country shimmered. People were assured that the nation's administration will be in a constitutionally correct manner.

It also meant that the nation could struggle under the British rule within the legal limits only. Nobody ever doubted constitutionally and legally bound movement and the extent of its success. At that time, adopting violent agitation as undertaken by Russia, Ireland, Italy and other countries was never thought of. At that moment, this English weapon was considered fit enough to fight back the English. The Indian leaders were appreciative of English liberalism till just before Mahatma Gandhi's arrival and depended upon alternatives of agitating within limits to handover the command to the leading legal experts among the public; but rarely a movement can be effective without mass participation. When the voice of protest kept on getting louder and louder in public in the nation, then the Indian National Congress was born in year of 1885. Founding Congress made it clear that leadership was no more limited up to local level but had turned national in true sense of meaning.

From the period of 1885 to 1915, i.e., nearly for thirty years, Congress and citizens had to face various types of problems. The objective kept on deluding even after the adoption of legal manners for the movement. Moments of frustration and agony kept on appearing during the sojourn of freedom struggle.

The British rulers were applying their authority in full to tighten their administrative claws. On the other hand, an alarmed and alert public was struggling to get rid of shackles of slavery. Then a time period arrived when the public gradually got disillusioned of the soft approach and started hunting newer modes to turn the struggle effective.

A rift of difference of opinion was initiated in the Congress regarding the approach to be adopted for the movement. One group wanted to protest in a constitutional manner while another group wanted to intensify the movement on the basis of public vote pressure.

The Congress maintained its unity for a few years but its tune kept on changing along with the changing conditions and demands of the time. At least, fissure emerged clearly and the government captured the extremist leaders in prison. A sort of vacuum was created in the country along the Congress also, when the extremist section was removed from the scene. Now the Congress was being controlled by the liberal leaders but a lack of enthusiasm and inspiration appeared in the Congress. After months past it, the Congress was left directionless. Later, a change took over this situation.

Gopal Krishna remained active in such a social and political time period and decided the direction of his life. His life began in the field of education and completed during the constitutionally run movement. His belief, courage, devotion and objectives in the hearts of Indians were permeated with inspiration. Gopal Krishna kept on stepping undoubtedly lifelong on the path he chose. His mind and conscious kept on maintaining the feeling of faith and dedication towards his ideals.

Gopal Krishna never left his ideals in his entire political life. His life was that of a devoted person. He adored India with all his heart. He also accepted that he became the true servant of India owing to the love for the country. Neither failures could ever deter him away of his objectives nor false pride for the same ever germinated in his heart, wooing to his achievements and success. He kept on being active till the last moments of his life like a true Karmayogi (i.e. work mediator).

Though India was chained in the fretter of slavery during the nineteenth century but in the span of this period, such great men were born in the country, who played a significant role in deciding the fate of this ancient land. There will be few countries across the world where such a great number of great men are born in such a short time span. India presented great personalities in the fields of arts, science, history, education, economics, commerce, politics and religion to the world. These personalities constructed sound foundation of the bright future of this country.

Gopal Krishna was born at the time period of such type of great persons, who were struggling to fulfil hopes and aspirations through law-supported and abided movement.

□

4

Star of Liberal Politics – Gopal Krishna Gokhale

Development of modern Indian political ideology has been linked deeply with that of the Indian National Movement. Before the rise of Mahatma Gandhi as a prominent political personality, two groups with two separate ideologies were seen in Indian National Congress. These two ideologies owning sects were known as moderate or liberal group and extremist or aggressive group. In the initial stage of the Indian National Movement, liberal thinkers like Justice M.G. Ranade, D.E. Wacha, Ferozeshah Mehta and Dada Bhai Nauroji, etc. liberal thinkers overtook the scene, who played a significant role in laying the foundation stone of liberal the political ideology. Gopal Krishna Gokhale was a pioneering liberal thinker of his times.

On the one hand, liberal thinkers emphasized adopting a flexible and open political point of view, while on the other, they talked of all-round but stepwise gradual development of the society. They looked at the British regime as different to the extremist ideology thinkers' point of view like that of Tilak, Arvind Ghosh, and Vipin Chandra Pal. Their idea of checking social altruism of Indians was quite different. These kept a different opinion of deciding and political and social aims as well as means to adaptor achieve the same also. If looked as a whole, the liberal thinkers were appreciating the British regime in India and were welcoming the same. They believed that only pace of modernisation process could be fastened only through the British rule. That is why, they were exclusively, emphasized on social and economic reforms because they used to believe sincerely sufficient social and economic reforms will carry no benefits. Gokhale considered prominent liberal thinkers after M.G. Ranade. Ranade played significant role in the development of liberal political thinking. As an ideal follower of M.G. Ranade and as a political Guru of Mahatma Gandhi, Gokhale provided a significant intellectual bridge between Ranade and Gandhi.

To understand Gokhale's political ideology, it is essential to understand how Gokhale's political life kept on achieving its pinnacle. It is obvious that his political activities were deeply related to his assumptions and inspiration.

Life Story

In a small village, Kotluk of Ratnagiri district in Maharashtra, Gopal Krishna Gokhale was born in a middle-class Chittpavan Brahmin family on 9 May 1866. His father Krishna Rav initially served as a clerk. Later, he was promoted and he became a sub-inspector. While Gopal Krishna was only 13 years old, his father died. His father was survived by two sons and four daughters. Elder brother Govind accepted all the responsibilities after the death of the father.

Gopal Krishna received his elementary education at Kagal near Kolhapur and he completed his education up to matric in 1881. He received his higher education at Raja Ram College of Kolhapur, Deccan College at Pune and Elphinstone College of Bombay. He completed his gradation in 1884 from Alphinstone College. Firstly, he decided to become an engineer, but later, he decided to devote himself to the educational field.

Few patriotic young men had established a middle school named 'New English School'. Being inspired by the famous nationalist leader Vishnu Shastri Chiploonkar, Gopal Krishna accepted the post of a teacher in New English School. The Manager of Deccan Education Society got impressed enough with his devotion and faith. They took Gopal Krishna as life member of the society. Soon Gopal Krishna was appointed as lecturer of Ferozeshah College. This college was also managed by Deccan Education Society. After this, Gopal Krishna continued teaching approximately for eighteen years.

Gopal Krishna was introduced to M.G. Ranade being in the teaching profession and from then on, he utilised his talent and capacity for social welfare under the able guidance of Ranade. M.G. Ranade had founded an association called 'Sarvajanik Sabha' to keep the common people aware. Gopal Krishna was appointed the secretary to this association. An impressive quarterly journal was being published by the society, which was edited by Gopal Krishna. A famous social reformer of the nineteenth century in Maharashtra, Gopal Ganesh Agarkar had started publishing a journal called *Sudharak* where, in English section, Gopal Krishna kept on writing regular articles for several years.

In 1889, Gopal Krishna attended the Indian National Congress session for the first time and after it, he became a regular orator in the Congress meetings.

In 1896, when Bal Gangadhar Tilak and his colleagues overpowered 'Sarvajanik Sabha', Ranade and Gopal Krishna and their other supporters isolated themselves from the society and funded a new association called Deccan Society. Gopal Krishna started taking special interest in the activities of this society. Gopal Krishna was sent to England to bear witness before Welby Commission. The British enhanced logical administrative distribution between the Indian and British government. This was his first English sojourn, owing to his superior performance; quite expectations were expected from him.

In 1899, he was elected to the Bombay Legislative Council. In 1902, he retired from his services at Fergusson College and he devoted the last thirteen years of his life totally to complete the political activities. During this time period, he was many times elected to the 'Imperial Legislative Council' and he was identified as an experienced mature leader. Specially, there was no match to his budget speeches, which were entrenched with constructive ideas. On the other hand, he never felt shy of criticising economic policies of the government.

Gopal Krishna Gokhale paid attention to the plight of Indians residing in South Africa after requests made by Mahatma Gandhi. From 1910 to 1912, he passed resolutions to award relief to Indian labourers in Imperial Legislative Council. In 1912, he visited South Africa on Gandhiji's invitation and played a crucial role to solve the problems of migrant Indians. In 1913, he collected funds to aid South African Satyagraha movement. Owing to extraordinary hectic life, Gopal Krishna died untimely in February 1915.

Ideological Influence

Political ideas and philosophy do not germinate in vacuum. These are born in a great environment. An ideologist is the product of his own time period. Gopal Krishna Gokhale was also no exception. The prominent persons and incidents of their life deeply influenced his idea and thinking.

Gopal Krishna adopted modern exhaustive point of view to life like civilised persons of his time; also as a person educated under the British education system. He studied Beacon's book *Public Speaker* and Beacon's book of essays, *The Advancement of Learning*, deeply in his student life. He learnt French book *Political Economy* by heart. In the same way, Bourke's book written on French revolution was on his tongue-tip orally. He was deeply influenced by John Stuart Mill's political principles 'Philosophy of Liberalism' and he was specially inspired by Mill's political principles as a history learner. Gopal Krishna was quite impressed by Ireland's Home Rule Movement. His ideology was shaped deeply different dimensions of European history and democratic development and his faith in there being a lot to learn from West became confirmed.

Among the Indian thinkers, M.G. Ranade influenced Gopal Krishna the most. Gopal Krishna always took pride in being Ranade's pupil. Gopal Krishna was specially influenced by Ranade's social and economic ideas. Gopal Krishna had a deep devotion to the sacrifice of Tilak and other nationalist leaders but he could not get attracted to their nationalistic ideology. This was the reason for his proximity to D.E. Wacha and Ferozeshah Mehta-type liberal thinker, who deeply influenced him for group's organisational management technique.

England's Marley and other contemporary liberal leaders also played a special role to shape looked at Gladstone and Marley with respect and he believed that liberal leaders of England will emphasize making Indian administration justifiable. Gopal Krishna's political ideology represents liberal point of view of his times. This was liberalism only which shaped his social and political ideas.

Political Ideology

Gopal Krishna was not a political leader in straight meaning. He had not propagated any type of political opinion like Hobbs or Lock nor had he authored any book to define his political ideology like *Geeta Rahasya* by Tilak and *Hind Swarajya* by Mahatma Gandhi. He had written sufficient articles, which explained his political ideology. In the same manner, Gokhale's political ideas can be familiarised through his lectures delivered on important social and economic issues at different occasions and his letters written to his contemporary.

Gopal Krishna's political ideology revolves around the prevailing socio-political issues much more than the fundamental political nation of state, nation and sovereignty, that is why, we will have to pay attention to his ideas towards contemporary fundamental political issue and his opinion to those issues; if we want to grasp his political principles. As the number of these issues is more than enough and these issues are getting complicated also, therefore, this richness of his political ideology is highlighted via his ideas expressed for the same.

Opinion of Gopal Krishna Gokhale towards English Regime

Gokhale supported English regime appreciating the same in India like majority of liberal Indian thinkers of his time. He was using two logics mainly to his reason behind praising English regime and its continuance in India. First, like other liberals, Gopal Krishna believed the establishment of English rule was the only reason of initiated modernisation process of the Indian society. Second, English regulated law and order system based on the principles of equality and affirmed freedom of expression and press through the principle of government elected by representatives even if the size of government was limited. All these points were absolutely new for India. English only have initiated the process of political unification of India.

Gopal Krishna believed that India could learn much from the Britishers. That is why, he said that we must accept English rule for a few more days and should progress in arenas of industry, commerce, education and politics. Gopal Krishna believed that if English rule went on for a few more years, then India will turn into a fully modern nation and will be able to stand shoulder-to-shoulder with other free countries in Europe.

Gopal Krishna thought that the Britishers will follow their liberal tradition to fulfil their assurances and as India will enable itself to run the government through self-dependency, they will gift India freedom. England's assurances kept on strengthening on the basis of the declaration of Thomas Munroe Macaulay, Henry Lawrence and even Queen Victoria herself. Though from time of ending of Viceroy Rippon's tenure in 1884 to August Declaration in 1917, the previous Viceroy and Indian secretaries expressed no intention that English hearts can be won over through examples of their liberalism and assurances of India's self-sufficiency. In this manner, English can be agreed to regulate Western political system in India. Owing to his faith in British liberalism, Gopal Krishna was supporting English rule in India.

Agreeing with the continuation of English rule in India did not mean that Gopal Krishna was fully satisfied with the British rule in India. For example, he was a hard critic of uncontrolled administration based on Curzon's policies. At many occasions, he had already commented that the British rule is more than the British people itself because it was hesitating to regulate England's political systems in India. Still he believed that India's progress was possible owing to the British rule.

Gopal Krishna believed that Indian history did not contribute particularly in developing democratic political system. In July 1911, reading his research paper in Universal Races Congress at London, Gopal Krishna said, "The national idea of political freedom like that in the West could not get developed in India." He opinionated that social and political system in the country should be reformed on the tune of the West. According to him, the European history presents the impressive picture of the social development of democratic ideas. So, it can be proved useful in shaping our freedom and democratic ideas. This aim can be fulfilled using contact with British rulers. Due to this reason only, he was supporting the British rule in India. Gopal Krishna gave his opinion in a letter written to his friend: "All of you can feel this point that whatever be the weakness of English bureaucracy but every English person appears disciplined and works to maintain system in the country and our public cannot grow truly without maintaining a proper system." In this manner, Gopal Krishna believed the British rule to bring about reforms in the British administration which was essential for the progress and, in this manner, he expressed his opinion to maintain the British rule.

Liberalism

As it has been already described that Gopal Krishna was a liberal ideologist, but his liberalism was a little different than conventional liberalism that was popular during the eighteenth-and nineteenth-century Europe. Firstly, it was important to understand specialities of conventional liberalism. Liberalism as an ideology can be defined as an idea bound to personal freedom as a policy and system of the government as a principle of social unification as a way of life for an individual and society. Freedom is a pivotal point of liberalism, which does not accept any interference in any aspect of life. Liberalism supports secularity in social field. It supports human deliverance from chains of religious fanatism and believes in freedom of mind. It supports free trade in the economic field, where internal production and external freedom to export remain free. It supports open competition where production and export of articles, materials face no restriction. Due to these reasons, it keeps faith in exploiting natural resources and policy of economic profit distribution among people. Gopal Krishna desired no interference by state in economic arena; and that state should play a positive role in the field of industrial commercial development.

Gopal Krishna being a liberal thinker supported individual freedom. But he was also of opinion that freedom must not mean indiscipline. Contrary to this, he believed that till few rights of self-rule will not be conferred to the citizens, no emotion of freedom could have been felt. According to him, freedom of expression and press was essential to experience personal freedom. This was the reason that he agreed for his protest against Authoritative Secrecy Act in 1904, that the Act was a governmental attempt to supply the government a weapon to control the press.

Gopal Krishna also supported the rights of personal wealth and freedom of contract. Commenting on Land Revenue Amendment Legislature, he said, "An ordinary citizen has a natural right over his personal property. If there is an attempt to snatch this right, he cannot be expected to sit idly. If a proposal to devoid him of this right is presented, then it will be considered a great trespass over his right." In this manner, Gopal Krishna supported the rights of personal property, individual freedom and freedom of contract, which were very essential components in establishing principles of liberalism.

Gopal Krishna advised to establish representative associations in the country for the security of individual freedom and essential civil rights. According to him, the first condition to improve relations between Britain and India was for Britain to announce clearly and instantly that it will develop representative associations in India. Although he was not talking about individual freedom for all, he was partial for giving this type of freedom on the basis of property. For example, he was in favour of allowing only such a person in the election of Gram Panchayat or village assembly, who paid minimum land revenue.

Gopal Krishna also talked of representing public interest besides public representatives in the legislative council. His suggestion was to include 75 to 100 members in the legislative council of every province. Illustrating Bombay, he also advised to a certain special representation, for Karachi Chambers, Ahmedabad mill owners and Deccan Sardars. Grasping community-wise division between Hindus and Muslims, he advised separate representation for Muslims. In this way, being a liberal thinker, if Gopal Krishna had supported concept of personal freedom on one hand, then on the other hand, he had also supported establishing representative associations in limited sense.

Gopal Krishna's idea in context of role of state was different than the conventional liberalism. The conventional liberalism advocates Free State and takes presence of police only enough for keeping a watch. It considers that an administration ruling with minimum of authority is the best of all the administrations. Gopal Krishna said that a state or regime must intervene for the progress of country's economic and social life. In this context, Gopal Krishna's opinion was much different than J.S. Mill's. Gopal Krishna wanted that the government must interfere for the prosperity of agricultural and industrial development. He wanted that the government should intervene not only in the process of distribution but also in the process of manufacture/production. He believed it to be the government's liability to fasten moral and physical progress of public. The government should lift 'non-essential bans' and should enhance the pace of progress. The state must not play the role of policing only but must enhance public welfare missions and should intervene in the country's economic life whenever essential conclusively it can be said that Gopal Krishna's liberalism was inspired by Mills' liberalism. There is not an iota of doubt regarding this fact.

Political Aim and Programme

The point of view of Gopal Krishna towards the British rule in India only decided his political aim and programme. He considered that India can be benefitted in the long run, if it keeps contact with the British rule. That is why, he always thought how to deepen this contact. In this way, the political aim he fixed was – 'Self-rule for an Indian'. The initial leaders of Congress were satisfied with the concept of good government, which meant expert and aware government. But like Dada Bhai Nauroji, Gopal Krishna also arrived at the conclusion that it was not possible to construct a good government without attaining the right of self-rule. Although he believed that English supplied a good government to nation through improvement in the law and order system. He believed that attachment of Indians with the governmental activities was very essential and this could be possible only when English people conferred the right of 'self-rule' to the Indians. In 1905, Gopal Krishna declared at Banaras session of Congress – "Now Congress wants a change. It wants that reign in India should be in the interest of Indians. This objective can be achieved only when the maximum room is created for our voice in our country's government."

In this manner, Gopal Krishna moved a step ahead of 'Self or Home Rule for India', not keeping himself limited up to a good government only. But what does the term 'Self or Home Rule', meant to him? Gopal Krishna's opinion was different to that of the extremist ideologist Arvind Ghosh or Vipin Chandra Pal had been thinking. Self-rule for him never meant 'complete freedom for India'. He wanted self-rule for India only under the British empire. On the other hand, extremist ideologists like Arvind Ghosh were in favour of getting India totally and completely free of the British rule. Gopal Krishna was not in favour of severing all the ties with the British empire. He also did not want to use the term 'Swarajya' like Tilak did. The assumption of Swarajya was elementary for Tilak and its objective was to attain complete freedom. Gopal Krishna did not ever favour complete freedom. On the other hand, freedom was the birthright of citizens for which no type of condition or limitation was required, according to Tilak. Gopal Krishna believed that people would have to acquire merit first to manage representative associations. People of East could learn ways of managing political associations of West through practical training, experience and application. Indians could acquire practical training only by maintaining better relations with the British.

Gopal Krishna prepared a political programme after deciding objectives of Self or Home-rule and also explained about devices and means necessary to execute the same. Many types of reforms were present therein his political programme. These reforms could be classified as:

1. Reforms with an objective to ensure increased public partnership in administration and greater public control. The reforms included – reforms in legislative council, appointment of Indians as Secretaries of States' counselling and executive councils in India, and gradual shift of Indians in public services as an alternate option of European agency in India.
2. Reforms with a nature to improve administrative methods, e.g. separation of executive and law authorities, reform in police system and other proposals of such type.
3. Reforms with a nature of proposal of change in economic policy so that the burden on tax-payer could be reduced and effective use of available resources be done. This included cutting off military expenditure and making land evolution effective, etc. and other such types of proposals.
4. Reforms that were used as a medium to improve the situation of common people. It included suggestions like expansion of primary education, industrial and

technical development grant to enhance sanitation, efforts to make farmers loan-free, etc. Gopal Krishna believed if Indians would use their collective energy to regulate such types of proposals, then positive results will be obtained very soon. At the Banaras Congress Session (1905), in his presidential lecture, Gopal Krishna expressed hope that after starting Congress movement, the first-time entrants, i.e. progressive and liberal group in ruling, will lead to the formation of strong public opinion against narrow and aggressive imperialism. He proposed a programme as encouraged by this very hope.

The means suggested by Gopal Krishna to apply his political objective and program were essentially legal. According to him, law-abiding movements were the only means to fulfil political ambition of the countrymen. The primary meaning of constitutionally supported movement was 'apply and request'. But as the last weapon, he had not refused the device of peaceful protest.

□

5
Initial Life

Gopal Krishna was born at Kotluk village of Ratnagiri district of old Bombay presidency on 9 May 1866. Gokhale family got settled in Kotluk coming from Velenshwar village of that very district. His ancestor settled in the nearby village Tamhanmala owing to financial reasons. Gokhale family has enough of land, which was very well looked after. But the fields of Ratnagiri district were not fertile, it being a hilly region. "Every year, at the onset of heavy rains, most of the water used to flow towards lower sea and the farmers had to await for irrigation problems all throughout the year. Ratnagiri was a naturally beautiful region, it being a coastal region. Here mangoes, coconuts, cashewnuts and jackfruits were grown in large numbers. During this period, there were no means of transportation."

Gopal Krishna was born in a middle-class family. Being a Chittpavan Brahmin, his family had moto, 'Be content with what you have got'. It is known of Chittpavan Brahmins that they are practical, ambitious, industrious and rich of impressive personality. This is the reason why, even if few in numbers, the persons born in this family have kept on playing a pioneering role in different areas. Peshva family that ruled Maharashtra for 100 years was Chittpavan Brahmin only. Many such public leaders were born in Ratnagiri district only, who carved their identity in Maharashtra and entire India.

Gopal Krishna's father Krishna Rav served at Kagal State (Principality) of Kolhapur state. Earlier, he was a clerk and later became a sub-inspector. Salaries used to be quite menial those days. Krishna Rav's wife belonged to Kotluk and to 'Oke' family. This couple had six offsprings. Whereas two were sons, the number of daughters was four. Elder son was named 'Govind' and the younger one was named 'Gopal'. Gopal Krishna was inspired to work selflessly by his family only. He maintained this trait of his clan and, on the basis of this, illuminated the path of his life.

Detailed description of Gopal Krishna's school life education and education at home during his elementary years is not available. His mother was not literate. At that time it was common thing for women in society. In spite of this, his mother was rich of traditional wit and was a very wise lady. She had Ramayana and Mahabharata stories on the tip of her tongue. She used to sing hymns of saints. Morning and evening equally, hymns, drenched in Godly devotion, were being sung at Gopal Krishna's home. This religious environment during Gopal Krishna's childhood influenced him to a great extent.

All the details of these aspects, like the place where he was born, in the school he received his primary education, the teachers who taught him and the students who were his classmates, are not available. His biographers have only mentioned that he received his primary education at Kagal. A reference from his school life is repeatedly quoted though. One day, a teacher assigned a maths sum to be solved by all the students. All the children answered it incorrectly but only Gopal Krishna's answer was correct. The teacher asked Gopal Krishna to stand up and then praised him. At this, Gopal Krishna started weeping. When he was asked the reason for this, he accepted that maths sum was not solved by himself but somebody else had solved it.

In 1874-75, Gopal Krishna was sent to Kolhapur for further studies, along with his elder brother Govind. Kolhapur was the capital of the Princedom and Kangla was nearby. During those times, only big cities like Kolhapur had English-medium schools.

The news of father's demise arrived while both the brothers were at Kolhapur only. At that time, Gopal Krishna was aged thirteen years and his elder brother Govind was eighteen years of age only. The death of an earning member in the family meant a halt of both the brother's education. Gopal Krishna's uncle Antaji took Gopal Krishna, his mother and four sisters along with him to Tumhanmala. Antaji himself was very poor and could hardly feed and nurse his own family. After living for a few months with him, Gopal Krishna's mother returned to Kagal with her daughters and decided to survive struggling. Under the changed circumstances, elder brother decided to give up studies and take up a job. It was decided that Gopal Krishna would continue his studies at Kolhapur. Owing to the reputation of the family, Govind got a job with a salary of 15 rupees a month at Kagal itself. It was very hard for Govind to bear the family expenses and brother's education with so menial a pay. Govind decided to send eight rupees per month for lodging, feeding and for the expenses of Gopal Krishna. In this way, the family had to survive under these circumstances with great hardship. Gopal Krishna was aware of his elder brother's self-sacrifice. The determination to achieve the target of life got strengthened in his heart.

Gopal Krishna used to spend four rupees per month for his food and anyhow manage fees, books and clothes with the rest of four rupees. He knew the hardship of his family. So, he always kept a distance from spendthriftness in every situation.

One day, one of his studymates asked him to accompany himself to watch a play (drama). Gopal Krishna got ready to go there and returned after watching it. After two days, the studymate asked him for ticket money payment. Gopal Krishna got startled. If he would have known that there was cost involved in watching the play, then he would have never gone to watch the play. But it was essential for Gopal Krishna to protect his self-respect. He paid two annas to his studymate without any protest. He decided to save on kerosene as a substitute for this spendthriftness. He started studying under the street-light during evening time.

Gopal Krishna passed matriculation at the age of fifteen years. But he was married even before this young age. There was a prevailing custom to marry at a very young age during those times.

Young Gopal Krishna had passed the 'Praveshika' exam in the very first attempt, although he could not receive any scholarship. Neither his name was registered in the list of successful students. The most mentionable point was that he had cleared the exam at a very young age only. Though he had an ambition and capacity both for higher studies, yet he was thinking it improper to let his family face hardships owing to his higher education. Gopal Krishna expressed his desire to take up a job so that the family burden could be lessened; but Govind and his wife did not surrender before his desire. Govind's wife put the proposal of selling all her ornaments for Gopal Krishna's higher education. This nation will remain grateful to Govind and his wife who sacrificed self to gift Gopal Krishna an opportunity to enable himself to serve the nation. In January 1882, Gopal Krishna got admitted in Raja Ram College of Kolhapur. He was a shy student. No great detail of his activities in College is available. He was an average student not an extraordinary brilliant one.

Gopal Krishna became famous soon in his college due to his wonderful memory. Shri Niwas Shashtri had mentioned an incident thus: "Often he used to handover his textbook to a fellow student and used to start revising the lesson. There was always a bet to pay one anna per error even if a single word was missed but no classmate could ever point out his mistake."

Gopal Krishna never had an ambition to acquire knowledge of English in the manner contemporary youth wanted to be its masters but he used to study English deeply. He used to learn the English lesson by heart. He could revise whole of the lesson through words of mouth without even a single mistake. Few of his classmates used to tease him by the title 'parrot' but he never used to mind it.

He completed his first year study at Raja Ram College in 1882. He had to join the college at Pune for his second year of study. He stayed at Pune only for a few days as he started the second year studies at Raja Ram College too shortly. He completed his first year of studies of B.A. at Kolhapur only and then joined Alphinstone College at Bombay for his second-year studies. Mathematics was his optional subject. He passed the exam with second division. This happened in 1884.

In 1880, Vishnu Shastri Chiploonkar had established a new English School at Pune. The next year Chiploonkar, Bal Gangadhar Tilak, Agarkar and other youngmen started publishing a weekly journal *Kesari* in Marathi and *Maharatta* in English. On 8 January 1882, few letters against Kolhapur's (Prime Minister) Deewan Barve were published. Barve was criticised in *Kesari* also. In the end, it was proved that letters against Barve were fake. So, in allegation of dishonour, Tilak and Agarkar were punished and jailed for four months each. Public sympathy accompanied both the editors and a fund was raised to help them out. The students started collecting donations. The students of 'New English School' and 'Deccan College' collected upto 400 rupees for this fund. Raja Ram College of Kolhapur also did not want to lag behind in this purpose. The college students staged Shakespeare's play *Comedy of Errors* to contribute to the fund. Now Gopal

Krishna got ready to play a role in it, who used to remain aloof of extracurricular activities. For the maiden chance, he participated in a public programme to express sympathy to the political objectives.

On going to Bombay for the last year's exam's studies, Gopal Krishna was very much impressed with Professor Hawthornwait, who was a famous teacher of mathematics and a 'true guide'. The English professor Dr. Welderwees Perth was also quite famous. Gopal Krishna was deeply influenced by both of these British professors. Both these teachers could not stay aloof of the influence created by Gopal Krishna's talent. Gopal Krishna started getting scholarship of twenty rupees per month.

In 1884, at the age of 18 years, Gopal Krishna received the degree of B.A., which was considered a big acheivement those days. Now he had many options. Should he secure admission for M.A. studies? Should he serve for government service? Should he study law to become an advocate? His few friends advised him to contest for ICS competitive exam. They also assured him to get money collected for this journey's expenditure, but Gopal Krishna did not like this idea. Maybe he did not consider himself worthy of this challenge or he did not like these services (ICS). He got admitted in an engineering college but finding much more brilliant classmates, he started feeling humiliated.

He stopped attending the classes. He could not find any attraction in the ordinary degree of M.A. He thought of studying law. In those times, advocates earned good money along with social prestige. After studying law, an option of being appointed as a Judge in the High Court also remained open with him. The post of a High Court Judge was considered the highest post for Indians those days. Gopal Krishna was considering studying law as the proper means to serve the nation.

Gopal Krishna started studying law in Deccan College at Pune, but he was worried of his sacrificing family. How long could a family wait for the return of good days? He felt earning money was essential to fulfil his duties towards his family. So, he accepted a job offer of 35 rupees per month in 'New English School' at Pune.

□

6
Preparation of Life Struggle

The happenings at Pune influenced life of Gopal Krishna much. He did not think over his role in perspective of socio-political incidents' sequence, when he decided to pick up teaching as a profession. But gradually, he kept on connecting with happenings at Pune. Grasping the demand of nation, the way his New English School colleagues wanted to fulfil their own individual responsibilities, likewise Gopal Krishna Gokhale also took oath in his mind to serve the nation.

The school he was serving in was no ordinary school. This was not a school where only clerks are prepared. Contrary to it , school founder wanted that self-respecting, knowledgeable and devoted youngmen be cultured. Gopal Krishna continued teaching in such an educational institute for 15 years.

The founder of this school was Vishnu Shastri Chiploonkar. He was a resident of Pune and he had studied upto graduation. He was transferred from Pune to Ratnagiri as a government teacher. He received a salary of a hundred rupees per month. In those days, it was considered as a good salary. He used to edit a journal called *Nibandhmala* in which thought-stimulating essays were being published. This journal was popular among the educated section. In one of his essays titled "Aamchya Deshachi Stithi", he wrote in straightforward words that it was essential to publicise education for rejuvenating the country anew. Government imposed a ban on this essay, taking some of its portions as objectionable. Chiploonkar resigned from service and decided to establish a school at Pune. In January 1880, New English School was founded.

While studying at Deccan College, Tilak and Agarkar were thinking on the same lines. He believed India will become free only when people of India will receive education of science, arts and ideology. Tilak has written: "He arrived at the decision while pondering over country's plight along with Agarkar, that country's progress depends upon education only." Tilak and Agarkar expressed their desire to serve in Chiploonkar's school. Some people made fun of both of them but a new consciousness was generated in minds of students. Chiploonkar had commented, "I will like to shatter the chains forever instead of bowing head before injustice." His invocation was influencing the new generation. Newer types of students were reaching the school to secure admission. But the government was keeping a vigil over the school. Chiploonkar used to be disciplined and controlled while explaining objectives of the school in his welcome lecture. He used to say only that the objective of his school was to make education available to all the sections of the society. Chiploonkar, Tilak and Namjoshi started teaching in school. Initially, Agarkar did not involve himself in the school as he wanted to first complete his M.A. degree. He asked for some time to be assigned for the same purpose.

Hard work and sacrifices were needed to make a success of this new venture, salary of exuberant youngmen was fixed in the range of 30 rupees to 35 rupees per month. They decided to open new schools at different places in Maharashtra whenever good amount of money got collected, instead of getting a hike in their own salaries. In this manner, they practiced what they preached, i.e followed the sacrifice-ideals themselves. This experimentation was being carried for the first time at Pune. In March 1885, Fergusson College was established at Pune. The same year Indian National Congress was also founded.

Gopal Krishna was appointed at the post of assistant teacher in New English School at a salary of 35 rupees per month. This amount was too less. He started coaching the students appearing for public service exam along with one of his teacher-friends for his family's maintenance expenses. In this way, Gopal Krishna started earning 35 extra rupees per month. The eighteen-year-old teacher was earning a total of seventy to seventy-five rupees monthly, which was considered the good amount those days. Managing time, he also used to attend the law classes. In this manner, he passed his first exam of law. He used to go to Bombay at weekends and to study in law college there. He had a strong desire to become an advocate but he could not continue study of law owing to certain circumstances.

The environment, in which Gopal Krishna was living, started influencing him deeply and gradually. He was introduced to enthusiastic young men like Tilak and Agarkar, who loved their country wholeheartedly. Later, incidents kept on making it obvious that Gopal Krishna's personality was influenced much more by Agarkar's as compared to Tilak's. Instead of Tilak, it was Agarkar only who requested Gopal Krishna to become a life member of school management and to accompany him. Initially, Gopal Krishna was apprehensive. It was not as if he did not care. Only he was thoughtful of the possible objection by his elder brother. In 1886, when elder brother Govind permitted, he got involved in its management. In this way, the foundation stone of his future was laid.

In 1885, Gopal Krishna delivered his first lecture in public at Kolhapur. That meeting was chaired by William Lee Marner. His topic was 'India under British Regime'. Speaking fluently in English, as Gopal Krishna presented facts, the audience was mesmerised. Warner praised his lecture wholeheartedly.

Gopal Krishna did not carve any extraordinary identity as a teacher. He used to teach English to fourth and fifth class students. It is not necessary for a successful wise person to be a successful teacher also. But Gopal Krishna was a very hard-working and dedicated person. He used to prepare well in advance for his lessons in the class. He never used to depend upon textbooks while teaching but when he used to explain poems, the students could not follow him well. Students used to feel that their teacher liked to use such tough chaste English words, whose meanings could not be grasped easily by everyone. The students wanted to get easy learning of their lessons while Gopal Krishna wanted to introduce the deep concept of the lessons to them.

He had to teach Southay's creation *Life of Nelson* while professing at Fergusson College. It was not easy to teach the Indian students this creation as it contained the description of ocean, ship and life of a mariner. Gopal Krishna visited Bombay and looked deeply into the life at ships standing at seashore in order to teach the creative book well.

In the very first year of his teaching profession, Gopal Krishna had decided to acquire great skill and expertise, i.e. hold on English subject. Gradually, he kept on memorising creations of superior literatures. He crammed Milton's creation *Paradise Lost*, Burke, Gladstone, John Bright and other British orators and lectures of parliamentarians. He used to revise crammed lecture at the isolated places and hardly ever committed any mistake while doing so. In the same manner, he used to memorise the editorial of English newspapers. Fergusson College was developing a superior tradition. Students were arriving from various regions. Very meritorious teachers were teaching in this college. Gopal Krishna wanted to improve himself as a better teacher and he always tried hard for the same.

Gopal Krishna was greatly assisted by the method of self-training. He studied literature and liberalism to enhance his capacity of his knowledge and analysis. He received a great boost through this type of study for becoming a public leader in his future life.

Gopal Krishna used to teach maths and other subjects also whenever need did arise in New English School. In 1886-87, the idea of writing a book struck Gopal Krishna in the class, while teaching arithmetic in class. Those days as well as later, teachers at Fergusson College were asked to teach at New English School also. Gokhale exchanged ideas with experienced teachers of maths, N.J. Bapat and both of them together created a textbook. Gopal Krishna showed the textbook to maths professor Tilak. Tilak liked the book and asked him to present it to a publisher for publication. This book was recognised as a textbook to be used in New English School even before printing. This book proved useful and popular. It was accepted by many schools in the country. Many editions of this textbook were published and sold like torrents of rain. The publishers started paying rupees 1,500 per year as royalty of book to its writer Gopal Krishna. At first, this book was published in English and was later translated into other languages as well. Gradually, Gopal Krishna's life aligned on tracks but the condition of school management committee was not good. This or that obstacle/problem kept on peeping ahead since the time Gopal Krishna had accepted membership of the association. It is essential to understand opposite current and inner current of this prime association that influenced life of Maharashtra, hence indirectly that of India, on 17 March 1882. At the age of 32 years only, the school founder Vishnu Shastri Chiploonkar's untimely demise happened. In July 1882, Agarkar and Tilak were sentenced four months in prison for slighting honour of Kolhapur's Deewan. On 24 October

1884, Deccan Education Society was formed. On 22 January 1885, Fergusson College was inaugurated. On 4 October 1890, Tilak resigned from life membership of society. These are the important dates of Deccan Education Society. Tilak and Gokhale rose to all India level leaders. Both of them played a prominent role in writing destiny of this country. Still a difference of opinions and ideas lurked between these two. This rift started showing up on their mutual relationship at the onset of initial stage only.

Tilak and Agarkar were considered inseparable friends during student life and after establishing the society. Both of them had taken oath to struggle for freedom of the nation. Agarkar was emphasizing on social reforms for political change. On the other hand, without resisting social welfare, Tilak believed that the society should be reformed after attaining political freedom. Both of them along with one other friend started publication of 'Kesari' and Maharatta. Tilak used to publish *Kesari* and Agarkar used to publish *Maharatta.* Several instances, mutually opposite ideas started being published. The rift between opinions and ideas of both of them started widening.

Both Agarkar and Tilak were advancing their steps firm on ideals of renouncement and self-sacrifice. But a cleavage in their ideas developed fast, due to choice of procedures to be applied to gain the ideal. It was essential to maintain accurate balance between ideal and practical. In 1890, Tilak had discussed this issue in his memorable resignation letter. He wrote that at several occasions, he suggested for changes and modifications but no care was taken for the same. He also raised questions of hike in salary. Should life member of society earn outside of it? And in this way, should he waste energy? Will this teaching work not be disturbed through his involvement outside? He posed such type of many questions.

Tilak argued that there should be no discrimination among teachers. There was a provision to pay 75 rupees salary per month, 400 rupees annual allowance and 3000 rupees as life insurance policy. At the same time, there were provisions of life time pay to life members. Tilak believed that since all the teachers are involved in the same pursuit, so there should be no discrimination of any type.

Severe rift in ideas was generated due to misunderstanding. Tilak wrote in his resignation letter – "It is essential for teachers to stop working outside or such a ruling should be made so that outer earnings should be deposited in a collective fund, as is done in missionary societies, to escape from hardships." Tilak wrote that new members can use life membership for fulfilling personal ambitions.

The background of Tilak's resignation can be understood by one more incident. When Gopal Krishna decided to accept the post of all public (people's) assembly/council, the moment of rift in the ideas arrived. On 25 July 1890, Tilak proposed to call a meeting through a letter written to the secretary of Deccan Education Society. In the letter, he wrote – "I know that Gokhale has got concession of earning from an outer source, but it was my belief that there should be a line of division between once a while doing ouside work and permanently doing so. As doing so is against our declared objectives, that is for which we have gathered and unified."

A meeting was called where Tilak presented a proposal to protest against Gopal Krishna's decision of accepting a post of secretary of Sarvajanik Sabha. Five members voted against it. Agarkar and Gopal Krishna were in minority vote. In the same meeting, the proposal was passed by five votes of protest/opposition against four votes in favour. Patankar, who earlier voted in favour of Tilak, changed his mind later to generate a strange situation. Gopal Krishna was free to accept the post and not even. The same year, a meeting was recalled on 14

October, in which Professor Kelkar put up a proposal to protest against Gopal Krishna's decision. This proposal was passed with six votes versus three votes. After passing of the proposal, Agarkar said, "This decision applies to all the members." Then there was voting to ascertain the members on which this was applicable. It was told that this decision could be applied upon Tilak, Agarkar, Namjoshi and Apte. In this manner, Tilak was affected by this fundamental proposal. He resigned immediately. In this way, the society was divided. Gopal Krishna had already accepted the post of secretary and this was to depend upon his conscious to accept or refuse or work at that post or not.

After Tilak's resignation, Gopal Krishna said writing a letter in the very same day's meeting, when he expressed his desire to resign, if Tilak would take back his resignation, after isolating himself (Gokhale) from the society. Gopal Krishna was told that his staying back in the society or not was not at all a cause for Tilak's resignation. In this way, Gopal Krishna took back his own resignation. Patankar also resigned along with Tilak, which was accepted. In this manner, the most painful chapter was closed in society's history.

Deccan Education Society continued its struggle in the field of publicity and expansion of education. Many educational institutes were established by inspiration of this society, whose members were following the principle of self-sacrifice. Leaders of the society kept on adapting liberalism, humility and harmony in an effort to avoid clash with the government.

Gopal Krishna and Tilak were great leaders of vast expanse beyond the limits of the society. After its nine years, Gopal Krishna established Servants of India Society. Then they framed a rule that the society members cannot earn from outside. If something more than the fixed earning is received, then it would have to be deposited in the society fund only. In this manner, Gopal Krishna regulated the principle of sacrifice in his association, though he could not follow the same pattern in Deccan Education Society.

After that, Tilak could not establish any such society where these types of principles could be applied. But *Kesari* and *Maharatta* had propagated the feeling of sacrifice among people. Tilak used to manage both the journals. Always he had to face economic hardship. He could not pay proper salary to his employees nor had he regulated any such principle of banning external activities in the interest of journals. Contrary to it, external activities were awarding power and prestige to journals.

Members of Deccan Education Society believed that making Indians self-dependent through the medium of education was essential to liberate them of foreign rule. Tilak, Agarkar and their companions used to understand grass root level reality the of country. He believed that the country could be freed only through sacrifice. What was the most important factor? Emotion of sacrifice to educate people or the same for gaining freedom only? Gopal Krishna had not pondered deeply on those issues till then. He was in search of a guide. He was much more influenced by Agarkar's personality as compared to Tilak's. He had also thought of separation from society but rift of ideas could not be filled even then. His natural, simple and straightforward personality is highlighted by this sequence of happenings.

□

7

Construction of Fergusson College

Activities of society school and college kept on running even after separation of Tilak and his two other colleagues, but future scenery was not clear to the people who were attached to these institutions. A cleavage in opinions also started appearing among them. Camping started even among the students. At such an unstable environment, Gopal Krishna had to hold responsibility. Tilak founded no more institution after getting separated. Tilak had assured that he would definitely come to teach in Fergusson College. But it never happened. He could not come to teach even once after getting separated from the society.

It was not easy to establish the old image of the society anew. Although joining of R.P. Paranjpe and R.D. Ranade likes of wisemen with society was being taken as an important achievement.

Thousands of young people got ready for service to the nation through the efforts undertaken by Deccan Education Society. To say so is no exaggeration that this very society prepared persons who led all the regions of Maharashtra. Many schools and colleges in Bombay Province were founded by taking this institution as an ideal. Looking with this point of view, the objective of the society founders was completed to a great extent. Gopal Krishna started teaching mathematics after Tilak got separated. Later, he started teaching economics and history also. It is said that teaching of subjects other than economics or history did not seem natural to him. His one ex-pupil R.P. Paranjpe has written – "Gokhale taught very carefully. He used to work quite hard to explain even an easy lesson used historical context. It can be said that his teaching was more useful than Professor Kelkar's for an ordinary student."

His one more student Professor T.K. Shahani has written – "In 1901, the way he taught Burke's creation *The French Revolution* was a wonderful illustration of his brilliance. Even a retarded student could understand the core of the lesson very well, due to the examples he used to depend upon."

These opinions about Gopal Krishna appear accurate, even though these are different from what Paranjpe has mentioned about his teaching of literature. Shahani has mentioned teaching of history and literature. Paranjpe was Gopal Krishna's student while he had just started teaching and Shahani became his pupil during the last leg of his teaching career. Both of them agreed on the issue that an ordinary examinee and a dim-witted student could benefit from his teaching. This means that Gopal Krishna did not remain unsuccessful in the teaching profession. Maybe he was not a teacher rich of marvellous capacity but he used to work hard while preparing for his lessons.

Gopal Krishna stayed with the society for fifteen years. It will be worthwhile to pay attention to certain factors of that time to evaluate his contribution. Gopal Krishna had written few articles in *Maharatta*. He was entrusted responsibility of writing briefs for *Kesari* through collected news pieces, when Agarkar started publishing a journal called *Sudharak*. There Gopal Krishna was appointed in-charge of its English section. Few of his articles were quite impressive but he was not a brilliant journalist like his contemporary leaders.

In 1886-87, he wrote an essay series in *Maharatta* about wars in Europe, which was appreciated a lot. The governor liked these articles so much that he became a regular reader of the journal. Except these scattered attempts, Gopal Krishna did not even try to take a deep dive in the field of journalism.

In those times, politics and journalism had a deep relationship. Every leader had this or that journal to gather support. When Gopal Krishna came in contact with M.G. Ranade, then he was editing a quarterly magazine of Sarvajanik Sabha. Along with social life, Gopal Krishna's personal life was also changing. He never left any shortcoming or gap in education and encouragement for his brother's offsprings. Gopal Krishna was married at the age of 14 years first time. His wife was suffering with a disease called 'leukoderma'. The pressure to remarry was put on him increasingly by elder brother and sister-in-law. Initially, he refused but later he got ready. It is said that he married second time only after securing his first wife's permission. His second marriage was fixed. His married life with second wife remained happy but this happiness could not stay for a long span of time. In 1900, his second wife expired. At that time, Gopal Krishna was 34 years old only. He had a son who died in young age only. He had two daughters – Kashibai and Godubai. Both of them acquired higher education under paternal guidance.

Gopal Krishna used to advocate social reform movement but he was not in the role of leadership. It is said that being compelled to marry second time while first wife was still there, he felt as if he was not fit to lead the society. If a person cannot practice according to his preaching himself, then he had no right to preach others. It appears this nature of idea germinated in his mind. He had a deep sympathy towards the social interest but he remained aloof and alone. It was a type of self-banishment. His Guru Ranade also had to face the same type of mental agony. Ranade married a woman of younger age after death of his first wife instead of remarrying a widow. He was harshly criticised for the same. Ranade used to advocate widow-remarriage but he had to remarry a woman, much younger in age, to him, after getting overruled by his family's pressure.

Gopal Krishna was a good player also. From 1887 to 1889, he kept on playing cricket regularly. Although he did not show any special skills of the game, he played tennis and billiards intermittently. He wanted to gain their skills like Western people. Once he had defeated an Englishman in the game of billiards. He also liked to play the games of cards and chess and used to enjoy himself with these games during the last days of his life.

Gopal Krishna was attached to drama or not, this issue has no information available. In those times, plays or dramas were considered popular media to canvass political and social matters. The statements that could not be delivered directly against the government, the same could be said indirectly with rounds and curves. Plays were also depended upon to strike on social ill-customs.

Gopal Krishna could not attract audiences through extremists and never had known how to enthuse them. But his lectures used to be sincere and deeply meaningful, in which more and more facts were used.

In 1895, Gopal Krishna was the seniormost member of Deccan Education Society. Rest of all the old members had either left it or had expired. Gopal Krishan's colleagues requested him to accept the post of principal at Fergusson College. He refused this proposal with civility. His external activities were increasing day by day. So, he never wanted to accept any extra responsibility. But Gopal Krishna was a responsible custodian, guardian a much more than just being a principal for the college.

Gopal Krishna remained even the secretary of Deccan Education Society for a few years. It was a challenging post but he fulfilled his responsibilities with utmost expertise. He had to knock at the doors of rich for collecting funds along with getting them ready to donate. The richer section of the society used to depend totally on the British Government to protect its existence. Even if a society was doing noble work and its objectives were even greater, but he had to bear annoyed glances of the government cast on itself. Thus, no rich person could afford to donate. The secretary had to look up to the government at one side and up to the rich section at another one. Native kings, industrialists, *samants* and other rich people never wanted to antagonise the government in any circumstances. Deccan Education Society had to essentially remove the government's doubts in context of its activities and students' career's building up.

It will be interesting to look that behaviour pattern of the society kept on changing along with time. The founder of New English School, Vishnu Chiploonkar had said, "He will not allow any English person to step in the school compound to spoil its purity, i.e. temple of learning he is building." After the demise of Chiploonkar, their declared attitude changed within one or two years afterwards. The college was also named after the contemporary governor. Once revoking, an English professor was also proposed, though it did not happen accordingly. Once an English principal Celeby was appointed the President of Deccan Education Society. It was not as if the society members were proud to connect relation with English people but they had to make the society survive. It was not possible to save the existence of an educational society/institution without the government recognition. Government used to aid only societies devoted to the government. Deccan Education Society had received government donation to compensate for its loss.

There were tough challenges facing Gopal Krishna but he accepted these challenges with his strong determination and promise owing to his civilised conduct and desire-oriented towards the development of the society. His path kept on being very easy. His efforts could collect such a capital that made hostel construction for the students alongside the college building possible. It was no mean achievement.

Gopal Krishna played a positive role in great field of Bombay University also. He remained a senate member for years together and kept on taking deep interest in its activities. He believed that senate activities must not rely on political basis. Event if the government was agreeable with this issue in principle but he was not able to follow in reality. Gopal Krishna had warned the government-nominated members on many occasions that they must not mishmash politics with education.

After Bengal Partition, the government decided not to teach history as a compulsory subject. It was argued that in England, its own history was not a compulsory subject for degree syllabus. So, even in India, history could not be the compulsory subject. It was also argued that majority of the students had no interest in history subject. So, its popularity was diminishing day by day. Lack of meritorious teachers to teach this subject properly was being experienced. Many arguments of this nature were given.

Gopal Krishna smashed all of these types of arguments. He said history was not a compulsory subject at Calcutta University. Still the students were taking interest in it and they were getting aware. Study of history has no link to political situation and any sort of revolt.

Director of public education, Sharp wrote letters to the teachers of various colleges asking them if history should be taught as a compulsory subject. Gopal Krishna could not take this sort of opinion. He strongly protested against the intervention of the government system in the field of education.

□

8

Entry in Politics

When Gopal Krishna became a teacher in Deccan Education Society, he was only nineteen years old. When he wanted to accept the post of secretary at Sarvajanik Sabha, Tilak protested and a crisis was generated in the society. When this incident occurred, Gopal Krishna was twenty-two years old. His personality kept on maturing in the later years. His thinking ability kept on strengthening due to the company of wise and brilliant colleagues. In this process, Gopal Krishna's personality kept on growing under the guidance of great men like Justice Ranade. Gopal Krishna could never forget Justice Ranade's influence.

Justice Ranade was such a leader of the society who created history. He was one of the founders of Indian National Congress. Many institutions of Maharashtra were born owing to his encouragement only. Starting his life as an economics teacher, Justice Ranade studied law and became a Judge at the High Court. Apart from the high post of the court, patriotism, brilliance and thinking power were filled in him upto the brim. Owing to all this, people kept on getting attracted to him. Years later, in 1942, Mahatma Gandhi had said in the Congress session organised at Bombay while putting a proposal, "Britishers! Leave India!", that Ranade was an ideal government servant. Ranade served the government but never accepted slavery. Mahatma Gandhi wanted the government servants to follow the example set by Ranade. Ranade was a fearless leader devoted to national interest. Such moments also arrived when the government doubted his faithfulness and spies followed him. Ranade was not a revolutionary. Instead he had deep faith on the process of development. He was called a 'political saint'.

Ranade was not a follower of narrow-minded ideas in religious matters like conservatives. He believed in prayer society, i.e Prarthana Samaj and was the main pillar of that institution. In spite of this, he never wanted to hurt peoples' emotions, having total faith in ancient customs. Many traditional ceremonies were performed/conducted even in his own family.

Ranade was a liberal revolutionary in social field. He conducted a strong agitation against the prevailing custom of 'child marriage'. He supported remarriage for widows and used to play active part in organising such type of marriages. He was strongly opposing many ill-customs, prevailing in Maharashtra along with Agarkar. He had been raising his voice against vices like cutting a female's hair (shaving of head) after her husband's death, neglecting girl child after birth and *sati pratha* (a ritual of making a widow burn with her dead husband's body).

Ranade was a faithful legislator in politics but his point of view was not passive. He used to fearlessly oppose wrong committed in governmental decision and activities. He used facts in his opinion and used to prepare strong public opinion through his powerful arguments.

Ranade also took interest in economical as in political reforms. He was the supporter of intense industrialisation. The principle of economics that can be applicable for England, why it could not be applicable for India? If India can produce articles and materials herself, then why should she be dependent upon foreign goods? According to him, only intense industrialisation could develop India fast. Economic policy-related essays of Ranade are still contextual. Gopal Krishna had accepted a great personality of such stature only, as his GURU.

After one year of Gopal Krishna, being a teacher there, a school programme was being organised at Heera Bagh in 1885. Gopal Krishna was entrusted with duty of receiving the guests and seating them. Being unfamiliar with Ranade, Gopal Krishna asked him to show his invitation card. Ranade had forgotten to carry invitation card. With self-staunch follower of rules, Gopal Krishna was not ready to let him enter without an invitation card. Secretary of Sarvajanik Sabha, Baba Sahab Sathe intervened in the matter and made Ranade sit on a chair reserved for him. Gopal Krishna forgot this incident and he found no necessity to apologise Ranade for what had happened.

The young school teacher became a college lecturer soon and started attracting city families' attention towards himself. Agarkar used to praise Gopal Krishna to people. Agarkar himself suggested Ranade to call and converse with the very youngman. Baba Sahab Sathe accompanied Gopal Krishna to Ranade. Ranade was highly impressed with conduct, brilliance and human consciousness of Gopal Krishna. It appeared as if two brilliant personalities merged together.

Gopal Krishna started to visit Ranade often considering him as his Guru. He started learning about politics and public service from Ranade. From 1887 to 1892, Gopal Krishna kept on taking lessons from Ranade. Ranade was a strict teacher.

Ranade had developed a clear-cut idea about what should be done to change the political scenario in India. His style of work included reading every document published by the government attentively and thoroughly. No document was unimportant for him. After this, he used to write comments in a very learned and witty style about the governmental policies and used to send the same to the government. At that time, there was no ban imposed in the government offices to join politics. But it never meant that English officers were pleased with fearless opinion of Ranade. Ranade knew of his work being challenging but his arguments in favour of this action was clear that Indian public should be educated and made aware of administration skills and government weapon must be faced back with its own weapon only. Often he used to say that it was time of public discussion, so his hard work was not getting lost. He felt that the truths, being brought out in broad day light by him, could make the world, liberal powers of England and Indian public.

Even if the government might not have benefitted by Ranade's efforts, yet Gopal Krishna certainly did. Gopal Krishna decided direction of his future life on the basis of those ideas only. How knowledge and faith can be mutually linked for public service? How data can be useful in discussing complex problems, how skill of ideas is more important than that of language? All of these tricks Gopal Krishna learnt from Ranade.

It appeared as if Gopal Krishna did not have much interest in his Guru's religious and social ideas. Neither he followed all the directives of Ranade nor he opposed his ideas like other people did. Instead his deep interest lied in his Guru's political economics. Once or twice, Gopal Krishna was linked to social disputes also. Once prestigious people of Pune were invited to a Christian institution, where a few English missionaries were to deliver lectures. At the end of the meeting, tea was served. In those times, it was believed to be a sin for Hindus to have tea, handed over by missionaries. One could even get ostracised from the community. On doing so, familiar to all the invited persons, Gopal Rav Joshi had opted for Christianity and he was going to declare this fact. Later, served tea. Then Ranade, Gopal Krishna and Tilak glanced at one another. They were not able to decide their course of action. Other non-Christian guests were also in the same dilemma. Some took only one sip, some threw the tea down and some kept on touching empty cups to their lips. Everyday was tense for them thinking of its consequence. Gopal Rav Joshi got full agenda of meeting along with a list of every invited guest printed in newspaper. All hell broke loose after publication of the news. Sanatan sect of society got annoyed. This incident was being discussed in the streets and lanes. Shankaracharya was asked to fix a method of atonement. All the persons attending this missionary function were asked to atone their sin. They were asked to donate four annas to a Brahmin priest as atonement. Religious customs were very strictly regulated in those times. Everybody accepted this path of sanitisation but Gopal Krishna among other 15 persons did not get himself purified.

Education acquired from Ranade contributed especially to this prestige earned by Gopal Krishna for his brilliant talent during later years. Ranade never liked to miss any fact even in a short letter or commit any mistake of language. He kept on working hard and improving constantly till he achieved satisfaction. To keep his Guru pleased, Gopal Krishna used to complete his assignment with concentration and keeping awake like a yogi the whole night. Ranade never allowed Gopal Krishna to stay at peace till he did not complete his assignment properly. Ranade also used to appreciate miserly. If Ranade ever commented on it to be O.K., then Gopal Krishna took it as a very big reward for himself.

Ranade always paid utmost attention to control his language while dealing with his opponents. He never used superficial or insulting language in getting swayed during political debates or discussions. He believed in defeating opponents using data and facts. Ranade had faith in using data and facts. Ranade had faith in using powerful arguments relevant to main issues, avoiding personal attacks. While Gopal Krishna was familiar with other traditional ways of dealing disputes being younger and immature.

Gopal Krishna succeeded in fixing his life's aim under the influence of Ranade only. He decided to devote himself for politics and public service and remaining uncompromised on his principles as a public servant and not to deceive himself owing to temptation. Gopal Krishna adopted qualities of dedication, truth, to accept his shortcomings and mistakes, self-surrender to aim and regard to moral standards at a very young age only, which transformed him into a quality public servant.

Ranade was a religious person. He used to pray for a few hours daily after getting up early in the morning. Gopal Krishna had mentioned an incident. In 1897, Gopal Krishna was returning with his Guru Ranade from Amravati Congress session. There was only this Guru-Shishya duo in the train's compartment. He has written – "It was going to be about four o'clock in the morning. I was awakened by the sound of singing. I spotted Ranade sitting and singing Tukaram's hymn creation 'Abhang'. He was singing repeatedly and was sitting in a praying posture with joined palms (as in 'namaste'). Even if the voice was not sweet, one got overwhelmed hearing a devotional emotion in this singing. I got up and started listening. It was a memorable moment of my life. I will never be able to forget this scene."

It is believed that Gopal Krishna never used to pray publicly but he was a religious person to the core. Shri Niwas Shastri has written – "He used to have deep faith in God and desired to contribute in public welfare work by God's grace. It is apparent on going through his personal documents." On 18 February, 1898, he had written – "I want to do the following things by mercy of Shri Guru Dattatreya:

1. I will practice yoga everyday.
2. I will study ancient and modern history, space science, geography, anatomy, psychology and French.
3. I will try to become a member of Bombay legislative council, supreme legislative council and the British

Parliament. I will make good use of my power through my all these ambitions.

4. I will like to deliver message to entire world after turning preacher of philosophy-based religion."

Shastri has termed this document as 'Prediction Document'. This is true also. He could serve the entire world along with serving India, if he could have got a long life.

This document was no ordinary description of a dream worker. Instead ambitions were exposed in light through this. One cannot feel surprised why he wanted to study geography, space, science, etc. subjects. His ambition to learn French as the language of communication in the West and its knowledge was essential to step on the international platform. Gopal Krishna succeeded upto a large extent in materialising his ambitions. Guru Dattatreya is considered as a creator, keeper and destroyer, all the three. Gopal Krishna used to worship all these three forms.

Virtuousness and greatness, strong ambition to serve, honesty and aloofness from all material are the factors that can turn any person spiritual. Gandhiji got pulled towards Gokhale's spiritual personality and not to his gentleness. Ranade, Gokhale, Gandhiji and Tilak, etc. all the public leaders were basically spiritual men.

In 1901, Ranade, whose ideals taught Gokhale to decide his life's direction, died. Gopal Krishna Gokhale was deeply hurt by Ranade's death. He wanted to write Ranade's biography. Gokhale felt sorry during the last days of his life, that he could not accomplish this assignment.

On Ranade's death, Gopal Krishna wrote – "On Rao Sahab's (Ranade's) death, I am feeling as if, all of a sudden, darkness has overpowered my life. World is grasping his importance and so people are paying me due importance but I am not feeling any happier by it. When a friend congratulates me, then it appears to me as if somebody is feasting me after my return from the funeral of a near and dear one. Of course, our agony must not be an obstacle of our path. We should keep on stepping ahead on the path of life faithfully and hopefully even after being devoid of our life-support."

Through these expressions of Gopal Krishna, we come to remember Jawaharlal Nehru's lecture delivered after Mahatma Gandhi's assassination. Gopal Krishna felt himself as an orphan but he never deviated from the path of his duty.

Remembering Ranade, Tilak wrote in *Kesari* – "The credit goes to Ranade if consciousness of protest and courage is appearing in Maharashtra and if an open debate linked to public interest issues is going on in journals and newspapers. Ranade built such an environment struggling continuously for 25 years." Then Tilak wrote ahead – "Ranade succeeded in his objectives because he followed his holy duties with patience, understanding and devotion."

□

9

Public Activities

Gopal Krishna started his political life as secretary to Sarvajanik Sabha when he accepted the post of secretary at society (sabha). Few members of Deccan Education Society expressed strong opposition and argued that Gopal Krishna would not be able to pay proper attention to college. For post of the secretary, there was a monthly salary fixed at forty rupees, which Gopal Krishna decided not to accept/receive. In this way, all the obstacles were removed.

Gopal Krishna started working under the guidance of Ranade, of course, on the basis of principles. Tilak protested the decision of Gopal Krishna but his protest did not prove effective. In this manner, rift of ideas was initiated between both the leaders. Ranade or Gopal Krishna, Deccan Education Society as society was already infested with debacle, Ranade was not attached to society actively. Although in 1884, once he was there in the council and donated fifty rupees after presenting himself on the occasion of college foundation day. But Ranade was always sought at the hour of crisis for consultation.

Sarvajanik Sabha played a significant role. There was not even a single institution at All-India level where public grievances could be pondered over. Before establishing Indian National Congress, fewer institutions were active in Calcutta, Bombay and Madras at local level. In 1853, similar type of institution was founded. Dada Bhai Nauroji had established Bombay Assocation at Bombay, and after 14 years at Pune. Its name was Pune Association. After three years, its name was changed to Sarvajanik Sabha. The aim of society was to attract government attention to public's needs and grievances. This society played a mediating role between ruler and public with due governmental permission. Its sponsor D.V. Joshi was a worker devoted to public welfare and was known as Sarvajanik Kaka among public. Though all the office-bearers of this society were heads of states and government bureaucrats, but all the activities of society were undertaken by Sarvajanik Kaka and Justice Ranade. Though Ranade's name was not registered in members' list, yet it was Ranade's brain only that was active behind all the activities of society. Society activities were not publicised much. Society was contesting the war through memorandum. Moment for movements and direct actions has still not arrived.

Gopal Krishna used to edit a quarterly magazine of society also, along with being its secretary. Twenty-six issue of the magazine had been published in their editing. A total of 49 essays were published in these 26 editions, out of which only nine essays were written by Gopal Krishna. All along the editing work, Gopal Krishna had to face a few obstacles constantly. The magazine used English as its medium of publication but the number of persons familiar with English was limited, so as to cause insufficient sales the same. From 500 customers, the number reduced to 200. Activism was infused in Tilak's breath. He and his colleagues believed in changing few tendencies quite fast across state, if not across country. After stable establishment of British rule, a new class of leaders was appearing ahead. Such persons were increasing in numbers, specially in politics of Bombay and Deccan. The richer section of society, newly and recently educated and government servants – these new classes were busy establishing a new identity in the society. Government was making efforts to connect this class to the process of policy-making. This was the reason why this class got active in praising British administration and following English culture blindly. Tilak believed that the section, which has turned faithful devotees of Britishers, could not be the means of Indian public's welfare. Tilak did not have any faith for people, who were following British culture. He believed in producing leaders emerging with national culture. He used to consider those leaders useful, who believed in country's cultures who was ready to sacrifice self to the nation's interest. Owing to these very values, Tilak used to keep deep faith in *Geeta*. He had faith for principle of doing one's own duty without desire of reward. He was not ready to listen to those who said that better sense will prevail Britishers on its own and then they will leave our country. He used to consider devotees of British as a new 'royal class' and never missed a chance to clash with them.

Membership of Sarvajanik Sabha was not open to all. Tilak registered extra members according to Sabha's principles and on 14th July 1895, in its common annual meeting, all the older (earlier) office-bearers lost the election. New office-bearers were elected for posts of presidents, treasurers and others, serving since very long times in the Sabha. Tilak did not express desire to remove Gopal Krishna but he himself did not deem it fit to continue even after being in minority. He resigned after some time. Ranade and his associates were not going to deviate from their path through this defeat. On 31 October 1896, they founded a new association called Deccan Sabha. Gopal Krishna was appointed as its secretary.

Tilak never expected of this chain of events. He even got worried after familiarising himself with objectives of Deccan Society. Sabha had declared to work on the basis of freedom and liberalism. There was nothing new in their objectives but it was defined in a specific manner. Freedom meant freedom from caste and creed prejudices and to adopt all the means for establishing justful contact among human beings, to say faithful to the ruler in a law-abiding way and handing over proper rights to public liberalism meant never to follow impractical ideals instead to act routinely, on the basis of truth and practicality and to balance a harmony using correct logics.

On 10 November 1896, Tilak sharply criticised these objectives through an article written in *Kesari*. He made serious charges on Ranade. But what made Tilak so annoyed? He believed that Ranade was instigating government by connecting freedom and liberalism with this institution to let the government deal strictly with other institutions as well. Even if this was not the aim of Ranade, still the government was definitely going to help itself with this rift.

At the establishment of Deccan Sabha one thing had become clear that Ranade, Tilak, Gopal Krishna were not going to work together nor were going to opt the same ideology on any of the issues. Ranade had never stayed in frontline of political activities but it was decided that his pupil Gopal Krishna was about to lead liberal camp. Even if in 1907, at Surat only, Indian National Congress was divided but its seed was already sown during power tussle between Deccan Education Society and supremacy of Sarvajanik Sabha. Two camps were already prevalent. Their difference of ideology was awaiting a chance to get obvious at the national level.

Tilak is often mentioned as an extremist leader. It can be understood correctly only when the meaning of Ranade's nationalism is grasped. Ranade and his companions believed that no development was possible without social reforms. In this manner, freedom is deeply related with social reforms. It is also linked to objectives of British rule in India. Tilak never had any faith on such definitions. He had faith in demands being put in the form of agitation. It was not as if Tilak kept an opinion contrary to the objectives of Deccan Sabha. He himself was an advocate of liberation from caste and creed prejudices and justice for all. Even if his opinion differed on the question of 'faithfulness', he never non-cooperated the law. If liberation means limiting objectives, then Tilak was not liberal. He took Swarajya/self-rule or Home Rule as birthright.

If looked at in the real sense of the word, then no leader can be called perfect or totally liberal or totally extremist. Those who were extremists also possessed some extent of liberalism. Similarly, liberals were also extremists as shown of a few occasions.

When Tilak held the leadership of Sarvajanik Sabha from that moment government stopped its grant. Hence, the association kept on lagging behind. Even with a person like Tilak, Deccan Sabha started sending government memorandums, and also started sending delegations whenever need arose. Gopal Krishna was devoted to his work with heart and soul. He was also sent to England to express India's representation before Welby Commission. This honour could not be achieved by Sarvajanik Sabha, though Gopal Krishna even mentioned his old relation with Sarvajanik Sabha before Welby Commission.

□

10

The Maiden Illustrative Achievement

It is said that Lord Welby was immortalised due to Gopal Krishna only. If Gopal Krishna would not have attached along, then Welby Commission and Welby himself would have secured a room in the dustbin of history. Welby Commission secured a mentionable position in the Indian history due to itself awarding Gopal Krishna an opportunity to bear witness before the Commission. This opportunity highlighted the Commission and proof of Gopal Krishna being an economist, state leader and patriot.

Welby Commission was appointed to examine work division between the British Government and British administration appointed in India. It appeared as if Indian public's ambition and aspirations had no meaning or weightage. The British Parliament set up this Commission under its own guidance to look after its own interests. There were a total of 14 members in the Commission with 11 government officers, who were in majority. W.S. Caine was among the minority group.

Few Indians were invited to express their opinion before the Commission. These Indians were Surendra Nath Bannerji, D.E. Wacha, G. Subrahmanium Aiyyer and Gopal Krishna Gokhale. Initially, the Commission was not in favour to listen to the opinion of any Indian. But owing to Dada Bhai Nauroji's efforts, it was compelled to do so. Gopal Krishna was the youngest member of the Indian delegation. He was thirty-one years of age. Earlier, Ranade or Raj Bahadur, G.P. Joshi were to go instead of Gopal Krishna but anyhow they could not go. They secured the representation of Deccan Society for Gopal Krishna, who fulfilled this duty skillfully. Gopal Krishna became an important personality in India's political and economic field.

The attention needs to be paid to the prevailing constitutional set-up while reviewing Gokhale's contribution. There was a legislation but its aim was to let rulers loose for exploitation and liberty to loiter India's wealth.

Gopal Krishna said before the Commission, "British public controls the British Parliament but the tax-paying Indian public has no control over the Indian government, instead the British tax-payers control India. What good can be expected of them? Would they not be desirous of gaining maximum wealth of a nation won? Queen's assurances and few other declarations are contained in papers only. Only one authority rules over India, which is called Secretary of State. Budget may have been discussed but is never passed."

Gopal Krishna told that the Indian revenue has guarded with zeal in a better manner during East India Company's reign. But conditions deteriorated during the direct British reign. The transfer of Company Rule to British Government directly proved contrary to Indian people's interest. The Company used to establish balance and harmony between Indian interests and British interest which were totally forgotten at the onset of the direct rule.

At the time Welby Commission was appointed, there was discontent in India over the issue of the British Government occupying new regions beyond Indian borders, spending India-generated revenue. The Britishers were being appointed in public services. English leaders were free to loot. Conspiracy to loot Indian wealth and to carry it to Britain was being materialised through laying of new railway lines. These were the main grievances. There were many other grievances too except these. But the real meaning of these grievances was like this – we are defeated people. Victor is overruling us. If possible, loosen the clasp. In those times, this was the very limit of law-abiding protest.

They believed voting on budget meant protecting Indian interests. But English rulers used to feel that this was striking of the roots of their reign. The English started war against Afghanistan and Burma (now Myanmar) to expand their reign. They had also expanded their field of influence in the east. Rupees eleven and half lakhs were spent on war and annexation campaign. This amount was taken out by the Indian taxpayers. It was not appropriate to burden India with this kind of expenditure. Gopal Krishna said that a huge European army was kept ready even during peacetime and India had to bear the expenditure of European soldier's high salaries. How could it be made proper. Continuously, new British soldiers were being admitted in the army and the expenditure kept on shooting up.

Similarly, in mid-1893, all the European soldiers were being paid 'exchange compensation allowance', separately. Owing to this allowance, European workers were receiving fat salaries. Gopal Krishna informed about this provision. Twelve lakh rupees in 1894-95 and thirteen lakh rupees in 1895-96 were being spent extra. He argued that there was no point in paying extra and separate allowance to the already well-paid European workers. But the tax-paying Indians possessed no rights and the Britishers who possessed this right had no concern about Indians' interests. The logic behind allowance payment was that the market value of rupee was much less than sterling. Gopal Krishna did not take this point as logical. In 1886, in this context, Gopal Krishna mentioned about a statement given by 'Bombay Chamber of Commerce', before the financial committee. This committee represented the interest of English traders. The Chamber had requested for the need to amend and reduce the monthly salary of officers receiving upto rupees 1,000 or more than it. Gopal Krishna mentioned a reference of finance commission appointed in 1886. Ranade was also a member of that commission. In 1885, European engineers employed in public works department had agitated against its reconstruction. The government had not put any ban on agitation, while there was a need to deal agitation for 'pay-hike' with a rough hand.

Gopal Krishna had also mentioned the government's generosity to the European traders to loot the Indian resources with both hands. Though railways were all over the country with the aim of easing army but movements, later it turned out to be benefitting the English traders. Private railways were being promoted. The English officers were shareholders of railway companies. These officers were making special concessions available to these private companies for personal profit.

There were also grievances regarding recruitments in the I.C.S. cadre. The Britishers were being appointed on important posts. Gopal Krishna presented data of working officers in Bombay Province at that time. Out of 157 posts of I.C.S., only five posts were filled by the Indians. Land records department had only six posts, all of which were filled by English officers. Out of 29 posts in the forest department, all were filled by the English officers. There was only one Indian officer out of twelve assigned in the salt department. On all the eleven posts in the jail department, the English officers were employed. The situation was similar in medical, sanitation, political, police and public works departments. The European officers were appointed on all the posts. Only a little presence of Indian officers was seen in the education department, where ten out of total forty-five posts had the Indian officers employed.

What could have been the connection of these facts with Commission's examination? When the Commission members asked not to mention, Gopal Krishna argued that all the problems were interconnected to one another. The statements irrelevant to them were very much relevant according to India and its problems. Gopal Krishna said that he did not want to suggest any remedy but wanted to frame the real situation quickly. He had a discussion with a few members of the Commission but all his arguments and logics were listened to carefully, although its result did not come out according to his expectation.

Gopal Krishna had to pass through a very tough exam during witnessing. He presented his side as an expert and responsible public leader. He kept his stance. Finally, when an attempt to prove all his arguments incorrect was made, he mentioned in his written evidence that increased construction of railways was being done to exploit. He presented this fact in detail. In an oral statement, he accepted that ease in transportation is achieved through development of railways. And it had become easier to supply food materials in places affected with famine. But the development of railways is not being done on the humane basis, instead for commercial gains only. Its fundamental aim was to exploit and carry the Indian wealth to foreign lands carrying Indian products at cheaper rate. Non-essential foreign goods were being sold to the Indians at a higher cost. His arguments that items imported from foreign countries were ruining Indian industries and cottage industries and weavers along other skilled Indians were turning unemployed.

Gopal Krishna submitted his witness before the Welby Commission on 12 April and 13 April 1897. He was satisfied that he fulfilled his duty with dedication.

□

11

Gopal Krishna Gokhale in the Indian National Congress

In 1893, the public in Pune was seen with unfathomable enthusiasm. Roads were decorated with torans (festoons), flowers and garlands. Pune was ready to welcome the great leader, Dada Bhai Nauroji. Gopal Krishna's excitement knew no boundaries. Then he was 27 years old only but his identity as a dedicated Congress leader was carved. Dada Bhai Nauroji was elected the president of Congress session to be conducted at Lahore and Gopal Krishna wanted to assist him being in proximity. He could not secure a spot close to Dada Bhai Nauroji in the horse-driven cart. So, he got satisfied on getting a seat near the cart's driver. He was raising slogans waving scarves and asking public to give way from his seat only. He was so excited that it was hard for a person to believe it.

In 1889, Gokhale and Tilak both joined the Congress. During that period, it was not easy for young men of their age to stay away from Congress due to patriotic emotions overflowing in every heart. A.O. Hume was calling for fifty such persons to devote their life to materialise the dream of a democratic government in India, who were selfless with moral courage and self-control. Gopal Krishna was one of such young men. Hundreds of young men had stepped ahead owing to patriotic feeling but there could be only a few counted ones of Gopal Krishna's stature.

Gopal Krishna or Tilak was not present at the time of Congress' establishment. Ranade was one of the Congress' founders. And Gopal Krishna had joined the Congress due to his inspiration only. Pune was going to have an opportunity to hold the maiden session of Congress. But due to outbreak of plague epidemic, the session was conducted at Bombay finally. Sir William Wedderburn was appointed the president of the Congress session. In 1889, the number of representatives participating in the session was also 1889 coincidently. Parliamentarian Charles Bradland also attended one session where he put a proposal related to the legislative council formation in India by presenting an Act in the Parliament. This proposal turned debatable. Tilak added an amendment to this proposal that members of supreme legislative councils. Gopal Krishna supported this proposal. If mutual relation of both these leaders paid attention, then this proves to be an isolated occasion when Gopal Krishna and Tilak appeared to be at unison on any important public issue. This proposal was refused. The idea of amendment germinated in Ranade's mind. Therefore, its support (of seconding) by Gopal Krishna was not in accordance to the code of conduct.

Gopal Krishna always attended every Congress session till the end of his life except in 1903, being busy in selection committee and in the 1913 and 1914, being sick, he could not attend it. He kept on participating actively in Congress activities and continued presenting his views on proposals. The Congress leaders used to get highly impressed with his capacity of expression, deep knowledge of the issues and his remarkable power of logic to make them consider Gokhale as a leader full of great potential.

Initially, proposals passed on behalf of the Congress were centered on light-natured frivolous routine issue. The Congress used to present few demands before the government. It depended upon whims of the government, whatever attitude it adopted towards the same. Through proposals, a consciousness was pervading public and people in the country and the world were being made aware of India's plight.

In 1835 the Congress session, the proposals passed were:

- A British commission should be appointed to examine the administrative affairs in India.
- Indian councils should be dispersed.
- Members for the legislative councils should be elected.
- Liberty to express ideas in the councils should be granted.
- Legislative assemblies be formed in North-West province, Awadh and Punjab.
- An adhoc committee of 'House of Common' be formed to think over the protest of majority in councils.
- An exam equivalent to I.C.S. be organised and age-limit should be relaxed in it.
- Military expenses be cut.

These proposals show up the issues to be protested by a representative in the assembly. Few Congress leaders were also members of legislature. So they had access to people's verdict for accepting such proposals. It was no easy task. Even ordinary demands took years together to get accepted.

Gopal Krishna had joined the Congress with new possibilities and potential. Aged senior leaders were very much influenced by him. Before the Pune session, Gokhale was made Congress secretary. Even Tilak was also its secretary.

As compared to other cities of India, Pune public's mind had livelier memories of Home Rule or indigenous rule. Even if the border of the British regime was being followed but patriot citizens used to look at the Britishers with scorn. One section of youth was showing protest to British regime in a violent manner. These revolutionaries had many fundamentalist supporters. Tilak never used to support extremism but he wanted to keep flame of national devotion burning. He detested mentality of slavery. He used to dream of freedom from foreign rule. It will also not be true that Ranade led liberal camp, thought lesser of patriotism than one led by Tilak. But Ferozeshah Mehta or Wacha could not be expected to repeat or relive Maratha history, would get inspired by Shivaji's valour epic or would make public aware through Ganpati festival. Tilak won public hearts by initiation of Shivaji festival and Ganpati festival during the span of 1893-94.

Both the camps were pleased that the Congress session is being organised in Pune. Both the camps desired to make this organisation successful. But it was not easy to forget internal rifts and differences of opinions. Ranade was regarded well but feeling of cooperation towards him was almost negligible. His supporters believed him to be excessively moralistic, social reformer and faithful to regime's greatness. When the point of organising the Congress session along with social reform movement at the same time. A section of people got annoyed. They started protesting against this. Debate arose around this issue. People started saying that they will not accept membership of Congress Welcome Committee till the decision to organise social reform movement was not decided at some other location. The date of Congress session was approaching closer. Tilak tried to make people understand, being Congress secretary, that it would not be wrong to organise social reform meeting but the protest of public did not subside. In the end, Tilak resigned from the post of secretary, feeling sorry for the protest. Ranade decided to organise social reform conference at some other place, with a view to normalizing the situation.

During these challenging times, Gopal Krishna undauntedly fulfilled duties of the secretary. He edited daily bulletin during the session and collected donation for funds, though he was not conferred any credit for the same.

□

12

A Moral Dilemma

Gopal Krishna stayed away from his motherland for five months, from March 1897 to July 1897, during his maiden journey to England. He had known England till now through books and papers, journals only. He was getting opportunity to view England with his own eyes for the first time. Dinshaw Eduljee Wache, who accompanied Gopal Krishna to go there for bearing testimony before Welby Commission, has written a detailed description of the England experience.

For Gopal Krishna, the social life of Britishers was unique. He had already learnt the mannerism of the civil society but initially he felt hesitated in the English society. Later, he kept on merging fast with that society.

It is a matter of surprise that Gopal Krishna had to stay for such a prolonged period in England. While starting from India, Gopal Krishna had fallen down in the waiting room of Kailym. He was struck on the chest but he was so shy that he did not inform of this accident even to Wacha. He kept on tolerating his pain silently. But on the third day, he informed Wacha of his distress under compulsion. Gopal Krishna was staying with Dada Bhai Nauroji but had maintained a distance from him. Actually, he did not want to converse frankly with a saint. Wacha informed Dada Bhai of the accident's severity and asked him to call a skilled doctor. Doctor visited Gokhale for examining him. He informed of injury being serious.

Anyhow, Gopal Krishna was saved. Treatment was started and after three days, he came out of danger.

Gopal Krishna was asked to take bedrest for a fortnight. The problem of person/attendant who would look after him arose. This was Gopal Krishna's good fortune that a very gentle lady was also along us at one of the staying spots, who belonged to the great family of 'sheridon'. She was very sensitive and kind. Mrs. Cosgrove accepted responsibility of looking after Gopal Krishna. Mrs. Cosgrove kept on looking after him till his health did not improve. Even no member of one's own family could look after so well as that lady did. Nobody could keep Gopal Krishna so happy. This was the reason for Gopal Krishna's quick recovery.

During his maiden journey to England, Gopal Krishna got introduced to many prominent British leaders. He was highly impressed with them. He liked meeting John Morley specially. Gopal Krishna always wore a Maharashtrian turban on his head wherever he went. In London, whether he used to visit Parliament or somewhere else, turban always used to be there on his head. Glancing at his golden turban, people's attention used to get attracted to him. According to Wacha, ladies liked Gopal Krishna wearing turban. Naturally, people used to identify him with this wherever he went. In later days again, when Gopal Krishna went on England's sojourn, he started wearing cap, leaving turban aside.

Gopal Krishna wanted to return India as soon as possible after bearing his witness before Welby Commission. In India, people were appreciating his performance very much. But destiny had proposed otherwise. Gopal Krisha had to face boycott by the government and his own countrymen, whereas he would have received appreciation and honour. It was the most painful chapter of his life.

When he was in England, India had to keep facing calamities during the same period. Plague was spread in Bombay at the start of October 1896. The same year people were screaming to be saved from famine. Bombay started appearing isolated and quiet due to two types of calamities but a new type of crisis was arising due to migration of people from the city. Plague infection started spreading due to these people. After Bombay, this epidemic spread upto Pune. Government could not afford epidemic to spread, itself sitting quietly. Governmental group decided to use sufficient efforts to control plague.

The English Government knew from its own experience that uncontrolled plague could cause great disaster. It was pressurising its representative deputed in India to take tough steps, so that no plague-affected could set his foot on the soil of England.

On 4 February, 1897, an Act was passed in Bombay legislative assembly, which conferred authority to government officers to take decisions for checking plague-spread at their own level. This right was similar to the one granted under 'Martial Law'. Indian people protested strongly against granting this type of unlimited right. In a flash, rules were prepared to execute the Act and public frustration and anger kept on enhancing. People kept on preferring to give up life instead of following those rules.

Bombay city administration started using its right in a law-assisted manner but the matter kept on deteriorating at Pune. An officer called Rand was appointed to take strict steps for controlling epidemic. He asked for military aid to get patients admitted in special hospitals, isolating infected persons after checking homes and sanitising the same. In this way, a war-like situation started appearing in the city. People were totally terrorised. All the military men were European. There was not even a single Indian armyman among them. Foreign army men had no sensitivity about Indian religion, regarding for rituals or customs in their mind. Tilak protested saying that step was worse than disease itself. He expressed protest and established a private hospital, where patients were being looked after very well but the government was not ready to receive criticism.

The public got terrified. Army men were not grasping need to prefer people's emotions. Traditional Hindu families desired to protect their homes and kitchen as well as sanctity of their worship houses at homes. But uncalled and unwanted soldiers were interfering their sanctity. People were getting excited but there was no one to attend their grievances.

On 22 June, 1897, Rand and his assistant Lieutenant Irist were returning home after dining at government house in diamond jubilee celebration of Queen Victoria's regime. Irist was killed at the spot of accident only while Rand was admitted in a hospital in the injured condition. There he also died after eleven days.

All hell was released loose on Pune then. Thousands of persons were dead. A huge number of people were escaping for their life. Houses infected with plague were marked. Two British officers were attacked two months after epidemic broke out. By that time, intensity of plague had reduced a little and few persons were arrested under murder charge and a case was registered. Then they were hanged till death, i.e. were executed.

Along with this, only various types of stories kept on propagating about English soldiers' tortures and barbaric attitude. Newspapers were reaching to Gopal Krishna with hair-raising description of incidents from the motherland. He turned restless. He did not believe much on news published in other newspapers but when he read an article, written in anger, in his own newspaper *Sudharak,* he instantly believed all the torture and excesses being committed at Pune. *Sudharak* had given a call on 12 April, 19 April and 10, May 1897 dated editions to take revenge and said that people should not tolerate injustice mutely. *Sudharak* had written in one of its articles: "Shame on you! Honour of your mother, sister and wife is damaged and looted and you are mute upto now, even animals do not tolerate injustice to this extent. Are you impotent? Your cowardice is more shameful than excesses meted out to you by soldiers."

In other article it was written – "Till now, these people were only stealing but now they are laying their hands on honour of your ladies. In spite of this, why does your blood not boil? How shameful this matter is? A person more coward than an Indian would not be found in the entire world? Why are you shedding tears quietly like an old lady? Can't you teach a lesson to your tormentors?" *Sudharak* was attacking Rand and administra-tion more straightforwardly as compared to *Kesari*.

Gopal Krishna was bearing his witness before Welby Commission on 12 and 13 April. Meanwhile, his newspaper was breathing out fire. His own city Pune was under crisis and was not in a condition to appreciate his performance. No Indian paper took interest in process of Gopal Krishna's witness before Welby Commission, where he emerged like a hero. But Gopal Krishna did not allow himself to be carried with prevailing distressful sequence of events in motherland and kept on fulfilling his duty faithfully.

After bearing witness before Commission, Gopal Krishna started reading letters sent by the friends and colleagues and newspaper attentively. He came to know prevailing terror. Professor V.K. Raj Pande, famous novelist of Pune, H.N. Apte, Sardar Natu, Pandit Ramabai had sent him written accounts of cases. There was news about a soldier who spoilt honour of two ladies, one of whom committed suicide. Gopal Krishna got highly agitated after coming across this written information. What could have he done? He was in England at the moment and requested government to check these excesses. So, that government was not ill-famed. He consulted his friends. Sir William Wedderburn advised him to raise the issue after confiding in few parliamentarians. He did likewise but without any effect. Then he got a letter about this issue, published in *Manchester Guardian*. In this paper, he described rape incident of those two ladies. An electrifying sensation infused England after publication of this letter. England society was considered very sensitive towards the issue of females.

Protest to this letter started, instead of attempt to eliminate this blotch after examining truth. English people were taking accusation by Gopal Krishna as their own insult. Government was not ready to give the matter chance of a fair judicial examination.

Bombay government was linked to matter directly. It got the accusation examined and informed English government that accusation was unfounded and based on rumour-generated hate and animosity. Head of Bombay Government, Lord Sandhurst sent plague administration-related questionnaire by telegram to five hundred denizens at Pune, to find out truth. These denizens were directed to send their answers by telegram only. Not even a single response confirmed accusation. Placed Gopal Kirshna how could Pune denizens confirm the truth? Terror was infused in the environment. Anybody who would have supported accusation levied by Gopal Krishna faced threat of punishment. People who were asked to answer back within 24 hours, people were not giving enough time to answer after cross-checking. In this way, administration had proved Gopal Krishna's accusation false. It was victory for the government. Everything that was published in newspaper was heard and seen proved to be false Bombay government notified that the soldiers behaved with civility in a humane manner with public. Could anybody believe this in any of the ways? In spite of this, Gopal Krishna was considered a lier. Accusation placed by him was declared self-manufactured. If this would have been someone else, then Gokhale would have questioned process and manner of public consensus, by sending letters to newspapers.

Even period of personal crises had arrived for Gopal Krishna. Even his friends and admires started criticising him suddenly. Indian Secretary of State proved Gopal Krishna's accusation as bundle of lies by appreciating Bombay government in 'House of Commons'.

Wacha was of the view that Gopal Krishna should not send letter in his own hands and named *Manchester Guardian* but Gopal Krishna could not grasp Wacha's intention behind this. Gopal Krishna had received letters from the friends on whom he kept faith more than on himself. Whatever could have he done in such circumstances? Would he have told friends that accidents described in their letters were self-manufactured? And he needed sufficient evidence to prove the same. Pune citizens were suffering through an ongoing endless torture. One of the spokespersons of Pune like Gokhales could not have remained mute after coming across plight of his city. It would have been taken as his passiveness, and insensivity had he remained silent.

Gopal Krishna had taken up right step according to circumstances. It can be really impossible to prove any accusation correct under power of foreign rule in spite of superior evidence. It does not mean for accusation to be unfounded. Administration can force raped women to refuse if rape was committed. That means, even after accusation being very much there, it cannot be proved as such.

Mental agony started troubling Gopal Krishna. He was a very sensitive person. He felt that his friends did not cross-check the accidents properly before sending it for printing. Government machinery was more powerful than common public's one. It was real hard for public to oppose government. Prestige of Gopal Krishna was at stake. He found his future apparently dark. Earlier, Gopal Krishna and Wacha had planned to travel the continent. Later, they abandoned the idea. During that period, he was struggling with himself only. What could have been the sense in travelling for him at that peculiar time period? On 18 July, 1897, he met Wacha at 'Brindacy', from where both of these left for motherland. He was appearing sad and was not talking to anyone, after getting up on ship. An ICS officer, Heeran was present on the ship who believed Gopal Krishna's accusation to be true. Heeran tried to console him. Other Britishers were glaring him with scorn and took that man as defaming the British army.

When the ship arrived at Eden, it was stopped at sea port. There Gopal Krishna received letters sent by friends. Friends had requested him not to expose their names to government that they had sent details of rapes in writing. This was altogether a different issue, Gopal Krishna would have told name of these friends. By reading their requests, Gopal Krishna was very much agonised. This way Gopal Krishna had shown courage to oppose excesses of torture meted out to his people; the same was not reciprocated by his friends.

The ship arrived at Bombay. The actual details post arrival not available. Wacha wrote – "After Gokhale's arrival at Bombay, a non-co-operation issue became history and I would not like to discuss it."

Description on two incidents is available in this reference. Bombay Police Commissioner paid a visit to Gopal Krishna. Similarly, Ferozshah Mehta's representatives also visited him. Why did the commissioner pay him a visit? It was no meeting to show civility. Also it was no case of arrest or search. If this would have been so, could it be constitutional? The letter was published in England, though it could be argued that this newspaper was also read in India. So, no question of area of judiciary could be raised. But before this, it was essential to register the complaint in Bombay Court to get search warrant. Neither any complaint was registered nor any order was issued. Was government afraid of bringing hidden truth, face-to-face, if issue of letter would be emphasised? Commissioner visited to inquire of future course of action by Gopal Krishna. Government's next action depended upon Gopal Krishna's response alone. It is said that Gopal Krishna responded that he will not act without consulting his friends in India. The Commissioner was not satisfied with this answer.

Representative of Ferozshah Mehta met Gopal Krishna on ship before commissioner's arrival and carried away papers related to his statements in England. Certainly, letters of Gopal Krishna's friends must have been included among those. Did these letters were handed over by Gokhale or destroyed the same or kept these secure with some person? If police commissioner came with a search warrant, then he could have taken back all the trouble-causing documents with him. No certain information is available in this regard. One point is of course mentioned that Gopal Krishna went to meet Ranade because he had blind faith in Ranade's guidance. No welcome ceremony was organised to hail him for the exemplary performance he undertook for interest of nation at England. Neither he himself wished to be decorated with garlands of flowers nor his friends and admirers wanted to do so.

Ranade advised Gopal Krishna to visit Pune and try to collect all the evidences to prove truth of accusation laid by him. After Gopal Krishan's return from Bombay, he informed Ranade that no such evidence was available. Now Gopal Krishna had no way left except asking non-conditional apology. Ranade had advised him thus. In this crisis of Gopal Krishna, Tilak could had been proved helpful. On 20 July of writing in *Kesari,* Tilak invoked public to write and send excesses and torture committed, write and send excesses of plague relief administration. Tilak wanted to get proof of excesses committed to be published in Bombay newspapers but government was wiser to be more alert. Before stories of excesses and torture could be collected, Gopal Krishna was arrested under charge of defamation on 27 July, i.e. three days before Gopal Krishan arrived Bombay, arrest of Tilak had been already made.

Tilak's biographer, N.C. Kelkar has written – "Unfortunately, Gokhale's statement was hyperbolic. At one hand, his informers were incorrect and at the other one, Gokhale committed mistake in getting this news published." Tilak wanted to prove soldier torture towards public, though even he could not prove issue of rapes on women as levied by Gopal Krishna.

Gopal Krishna's apology was published in *Times of India* and *Manchester Guardian* on 4 August, 1897. Apology request was lengthy and detailed, where even such people like army, were begged of pardon, which was not required at all. The last leg of apology was agonising. Gopal Krishna had written "I had criticised during such times while plague relief officer, Mr. Rand was lying in hospital being seriously injured and he needed sympathy and respect from all around him. Still now, I can feel the scornful situation. I have brought myself in, owing to my action. I lead enhanced His Excellency Governor's worries while he was thinking over elimination of this calamity. It also feels that at a time when liberal English people will be appreciating me, I unwontedly accused English soldiers, devoted to fulfil their duty. Once more I beg His Excellency Governor, members of plague committee, and soldiers connected with plague campaign pardon me."

In this way, an agonising chapter of Gopal Krishna's life ended. He begged pardon after accusing. This point could be accepted as logical but people deemed praise of soldiers as uncalled and unnecessary and as unfit. Besides this, he was expected to be fearless, generous and courageous. People felt bad of a leader of his stature begging of pardon. Even before this, Tilak and Agarkar had apologised unconditionally for publishing fake letters in Kolhapur case.

But most of the people and his intimate friends had not felt it correct that he appreciated services rendered by soldiers while begging for pardon in so humble language. People had tolerated torture by the soldiers during epidemic. If Gopal Krishna would have faced a trial, then people would have felt better. But Gopal Krishna was made of another clay. He could not have insisted a point, which was impossible to be proved. If one had to apologise, then according to him, it should had come from the heart.

What was the reaction of apology in India and Britain? Bombay Governor Lord Sand Hurst did not mention apology episode with grace at Bombay legislative council. Sand Hurst did not even mention Gokhale's name. In Lord Sand Hurst's statement, he advised Gopal Krishna to frame such charges in India only, if it is imperative for him to do so. So as to in case of accusation being incorrect, the same could be contested. Sand Hurst took two years to change his attitude. During later years, again plague spread its terror at Pune. During that time span, Gopal Krishna dedicated himself with great devotion and kept enquiring people's well-being door-to-door. In 1899, Lord Sand Hurst commented, "There is no one as hardworking, kind and sympathetic amidst workers for plague prevention like professor Gokhale." People of England presented wider generosity than Lord Sand Hurst. Morley had roared with laughter while mentioning this incident to Wederburn and Huemann and had asked Gopal Krishna not to lose heart. Hume had said, "I do not accept this incident seriously. Don't think at all in vain that our relation with you have broken up. So do not beg pardon. We take you as a person faithful to this objective only and I want to help you in every way possible to support you."

Gopal Krishna felt that Dada Bhai Nauroji had to suffer shame in Parliament due to him. His letter written to Dada Bhai was heart-touching. Two days after apologising, Gopal Krishna had said, "Government has taken its guild off before my arrival here and Russian government started playing in it instead. Such a terror of arrest and exile was ruled in Pune that it was not possible only more for anyone to tell the truth. Government had already decided against examination of truth, through an independent commission. In those circumstances, I had no way left except going back on my accusation. This is the reason I bowed before circumstances and raised my step, according to the best advice. I realise that my this step has damaged our great aim immensely."

Dada Bhai Nauroji had told him in response, "Follow your duty faithfully. I am with you in your prevailing crisis. After this agonising experience, never forget to ponder peacefully and patiently, before taking a decision. There is no need for you to get disappointed."

Gopal Krishna had written to opt for renunciation from public life in letters to few friends at England. Being sensitive and emotional, he never wanted to effect national interest due to himself. His well-wishers forbade him of renouncing public life. Renouncing public life was not a new idea in life of Gopal Krishna. On 8 February, 1896, before departing for England and after apology episode, he told GP Joshi in letter, "I have been disappointedly bored of Pune's public life. Recent occurrences have opened my eyes and I want to lead a peaceful life after getting free of public duties. Intermittently, idea of renunciation used to cross his mind, which could not stay there permanently."

Apology episode had cast a deep influence over society. Gopal Krishna's admirer and editor of *Gyan Prakash,* Vasudev Govind Apte said that nation was dishonored by Gopal Krishna's conduct. Gopal Krishna got hurt with his admirer's comment. But soon hope permeated his heart. He had answered, "As I am accused of an incorrect conduct, so one day I will fetch back my country's honour as a compensation than organiser like you, who would like to see, dying me, will be compelled to appreciate me."

□

13

In Bombay Legislative Assembly

Happiness of Gopal Krishna knew no bounds when in 1899, he came to know about winning election of Bombay legislative council. This was his first successful achievement followed by many other ones. He was declared as a person, capable to contest legal fight with government, owing to his performance before Welby Commission. Apology episode was almost already forgotten and government has also started respecting him forgetting its earlier annoyance. Government was impressed with his brilliance and devotion. Gopal Krishna had turned natural and simply easy like earlier. Enhanced service, struggle and dedication towards national interests had become his life's objective. Ranade was still there for his assistance and guidance.

In those times, government representatives were in majority in provincial council. Even direct election was not held for the selected seats. There were six districts in central divisions of Bombay Presidency. Here there was provision of a single seat and local district boards had to elect a representative for this seat. Gopal Krishna wanted to win from that seat only. In 1895 and 1897, Tilak had won election twice from this seat. In later years, he was sentenced for one-and-a-half year's imprisonment in reference of defamation case. Later six months imprisonment was reduced to free him of prison on 6 September, 1898. Tilak could have chosen to win election third time from this seat only to show public faith for himself. He tried to make an estimate of District Board Members' letters. Tilak came to know that members never wanted to annoy government in any way, even if they had felt sympathy for himself. Tilak abandoned the idea of contesting election. In this manner, Gopal Krishna's path became lighted and he easily won the election. His performance at the board was in practice, a rehearsal performance to be held at huge platform of Imperial Legislative Council.

Gopal Krishna had never remained a mute spectator as a member of legislative council. He made everybody aware of his presence even after himself being a new entrant. He used to take deep interest in proceedings and always intervened in an effective manner. He had great grasping power of Parliamentary (affairs) politics.

At Bombay Legislative Council, Gopal Krishna exhibited deep interest in the three problems – famine, Land Requisition Act and procedures in municipalities. Farmers of province could still not emerge out of ill-effects owing to furious famine of 1896. Gopal Krishna, during witness before Welby Commission, had mentioned how government was taking amount of money out of a fund, fixed for famine relief to grant it to loss-making private railway companies. He sent many memorandums as secretary to Sarvajanik Sabha and Deccan Sabha and had witnessed plight of distressed public with his own eyes and through meeting the public.

Famine policy was existing since the last so many years. But it was being executed properly. Objective of government might have been virtuous but needed to be executed. Gopal Krishna seized first opportunity to review. He did so expertly. According to statute book, minimum relief program was assured but could not be executed due to ill-administration. Gokhale protested of arranging relief work far from famine-affected villages. Gokhale argued that farmers or labourers could not stay away of their homes for long. Apart from this, there was a threat of epidemic spread owing to convergence of big population chunks at the same place. So, Gopal Krishna advised to establish cottage industries in famine-affected area so as to make people self-reliant. Labourers were made to toil hard under the scheme. 'Food for Work-Famine-affected labourers had no power to toil so hard. In this manner, governmental target of famine relief was not being materialised.' If labourers failed to properly complete a task then governmental officials used to charge fine. Pointing out shortcomings of scheme 'Food for Work', Gopal Krishna had told that Bombay government was introducing excessive narrow-heartedness as compared to other governments. This code was good on papers but its execution was being followed in an incorrect manner. Humane aspect must be taken care of while conducting such relief campaigns.

Gopal Krishna was considered expert of famine relief affairs all his life due to his personal sympathy to famine-affected population and his knowledge of all the aspects of famine code. His role influenced governmental policies and whatever positive changes could be brought about, made public thank him.

During those years, Maharashtra had to face many calamities. Famine plague, Hindu-Muslim riots, Crowford Scandal and few other incidents shook the people. Every year, plague caused lots of people to die. At one hand, there was a let loose free government, not ready to tolerate even ordinary protest, on the other hand, were public leaders divided among themselves only. Ordinary people had to survive with fierce difficulty while no say of hope was held in sight. Frustration, anger and repulsion of people against government was shooting up day by day. Still any possibility to bring a positive change was not visible. At that moment, such constructive ideologists were needed, who could guide public correctly grasping their emotions. Gopal Krishna was one of those ideologists.

On 30 May, 1901, Bombay government presented a land-related Act in legislative council. It remained contained in files only as non-government members protested it very strongly. This Act was bitterly protested by press, political organisation and farmers. Tilak wrote many articles in *Kesari* to protest government and to support attitude of non-governmental members.

In Bombay Presidency, small and big landowners were selling land to moneylenders due to famine-related compulsions and other causes. All around a criticism of compulsive land sale by farmers drowned in loan was prevailing. This way number of landless farmers was increasing gradually. Government had put an 'Act' in place to check this land sale. The Act had provision that landowner could mortgage his crop to lender but could not sell it. Government considered it a way to protect land farmers but issue of land revenue to be paid was overlooked. Farmers used to receive cash through land mortgage with moneylender and used to pay government its revenue, if land sale was banned then government used to occupy land due to non-payment of its revenue. In exchange, its landowner was allowed land-allotment for one year with the condition that he would pay rest of the money. In case of non-payment of this due amount, there was regulated rule to disown farmer of his land.

That meant that the solution given by government for loan issue was worse than agony of loan itself. Gopal Krishna wanted government to provide sound land reforms so that farmers could be assisted to enhance yield. In this way, farmers could have escaped moneylenders' claws. They could had tried to completely emerge out of loan through formation of cooperative societies.

Gopal Krishna had pondered this problem deeply and his suggestions for its remedy were very useful. He suggested for repealing this Act, there was a need to examine this problem anew. He did not agree with governmental opinion of unexpected rise in poverty and loan due to erstwhile Mogul reign. He criticised the uncalled for urgency in presenting this Act and not informing about it formally. Government argued that handful of supporters to moneylenders had started opposition to this Act. Crushing this false accusation, Gopal Krishna told, "I believe this Act to damage to the interests of moneylender will be done at all. This is the reason I take it as my duty to protest the Act."

Gopal Krishna was perceiving the crisis being generated in this case. Act was passed. He said, "The aim of this Act is the governmentalisation of the land, which is against interest of local people." Suggesting constructively, he said "Government may begin with a small region, if it wanted to test any experimentation, government can open agricultural banks to accept loan burden of farmers. This only government can stop land-sale by a ban."

Gopal Krishna's qualities of presenting facts, debating on the basis of government rules and giving new suggestions on the basis of his point of view. But even after non-governmental members' protests, government passed the Act. Ferozshah Mehta walked out of legislative council to register their protest. Gopal was also present among them. Gopal Krishna's suggestions were so accurate regarding establishment of cooperative lender banks and land mortgage bank that later government did establish such type of banks. Gopal Krishna belonged to faith that courage to struggle must not be lost even after a defeat.

While Gopal Krishna was a member of Bombay Legislative Council, at the same time, District municipality law was being amended. He was not a member at the time legislation was passed but legislation was under consideration with selection committee by the time he was elected. He was selected a member of this selection committee. He strongly protested proposal of community-wise representation in municipalities. He believed even society was possible but there should be no such difference before law/legislation/constitution. His protest was paid no attention and the provision to represent community-wise was maintained in a municipality.

As a member of legislative council, Gopal Krishna used to introduce himself through deep analysis, clear-cut expression and civilised conduct. He always presented his points keeping interests of lower classes in society in mind. He spoke what he felt in heart. When government granted the liberty of free sale liquor and the poor started becoming wine addicts; then he demanded complete ban on free sale of liquor to save poor. He believed that government was overlooking plight of poor against greed of free-sale-generated revenue.

Even during membership of Bombay Legislative Assembly, Gopal Krishna had kept on teaching at Fergusson College. In 1902, he got ready to retire from teaching profession. Activities for expansion of Fergusson College were assisted by his election in legislative council. Gopal Krishna could not have limited himself now upto two activities only. Public, university, municipality, all of these fields were looking at him expectantly. With the passage of time, even government kept on being impressed with his merit and capabilities and potential. Government started to grasp that it could not run its activities without Gokhale. The influence of his persona was also enhancing along with the passage of time.

□

14
In the Imperial Legislative Council

In January 1901, when Ranade died, then Gopal Krishna felt like an orphan. Ranade was like his father also and not only a Guru. One day before Ranade's demise, Gopal Krishna had requested Ferozshah Mehta by writing a letter that he must once get a chance to become a member in Imperial Legislative Council.

He had written in a letter that he was about to retire from his services at Fergusson College. This request was made keeping in his view to devote rest of his life to Indian political field service. His wife was already died. He was to receive an income of 15 rupees per month as salary and 30 rupees per month from college as pension. He wanted to serve the nation. Appreciating merit and prestige of Ferozshah Mehta, he had written, "I am requesting you that I am not desirous of prestige owing to personal ambition only." The storm that turbulated his life in 1897 had left indelible marks and injury. Then Manchergee Bhannagri had criticised him on 'House of Commons'. Gopal Krishna had written, "I had sworn the very night, I read this news. I sworn in that I will compensate for my mistake by dedicating my life for political objectives".

Mehta got impressed after reading his young friend and meritorious colleague's letter and it produced desired result to Gokhale. Other people were also there in race of membership but Mehta made everybody agree to nominate

Gopal Krishna without any opposition. In the beginning of 1902, at the age of 36 years, Gopal Krishna was selected member of Imperial Legislative Council. Later, he received honour of being its member three times.

Those days three types of people were acting in Maharashtra. First type included Ranade who had served in public life since long with his wonderful intelligence but he had never been active in any council or public platform. Tilak had sacrificed his life for common public. Still he had not received honour of being a successful parliamentarian. He struggled hard in his chosen field. At the same time, Gopal Krishna never desired to use public platform to attack the rulers. In this manner, he became an ideal representative for legislative assembly.

In course of 1902 to 1911, Gopal Krishna delivered eleven lectures on budget and other 36 important lectures. Specially there he spoke on finances and country's economic system. People were left amazed. His lectures till now had a historical importance. The way he used to prepare his lectures made his lectures memorable.

The prominent topics out of the ones he lectured on were – The Official Secret Act, Indian University Act, Cooperative Credit Societies Act, Objectionable Meeting Act, Press Bill, Loan Deduction, Railway Finances, Increase in Public Expenditure, Excise Tax on Cotton, Export Tax on Sugar, Public Services Tax, Fit Minimum Income, Marriage Act, Gold Currency, Fundamental Education Act, Basic Education Act, deep studies, liberal points of view and national interest, all of these were clearly reflected in his lectures.

In his budget speeches, he threw light on salt-tax, military expenditure, currency, indigenisation of services, tax, etc., and other related provisions. In his lectures, he emphasised that government was making India available on answerable responsible rule; was stripping local people off their fundamental rights; was not treating people with justful equality; was overlooking their civil rights, and was not presenting economic and industrial development to India. In his opinion, British rulers were unstoppable who were exploiting poor public of India to benefit their own country. This was the reason that majority of Indians were compelled to pass life like slaves under darkness of poverty. He had said that no civilised government can allow its public stay illiterate and devoid of fundamental rights. Soul of India was getting lost, self-pride was being sabotaged and industrial dexterity was disappearing fast.

Gopal Krishna used to adopt constitutional mode in this struggle against bureaucracy. He always presented his side on the basis of accurate data so that a deep impression of his arguments could be cast on addressee. He had deep faith in British justice and idea of equality. He always used to oppose injustice on foresaid base. He was highly optimistic. Criticism could neither weaken him nor could shake him.

The first budget lecture of Gopal Krishna turned out very important due to his broad-minded view and effective facts. In his lecture, decision to increase tax was criticised and worry about increasing poverty of population in country were expressed. His argument was like the time when Curzon's government's profit was shooting up, the decision to increase tax was unfair. Government was misusing profits and was totally overlooking public interest.

Next year, in his lectures, when Gopal Krishna asked thirty-three crore rupees profit collecting government to reduce tax on salt and cotton and to increase income tax rebate limit from 500 rupees to 1,000 rupees. Government accepted his demands regarding salt and income tax but excise duty on cotton remained the same. Government was compelled to change its decision, only to the powerful argument of Gopal Krishna. Though same concessions were also being demanded by the Indian National Congress.

The Indian Government was following Britain government's matter of excise duty on cotton. The Government was encouraging free trade to benefit textile industries of Manchester and Lancashire. In this way, the

Indian textile industry was also being profited a little. The Government had levied excise duty on cotton to keep the Indian textile industry devoid of profit. It meant the Government was discouraging the Indian textile industry instead of encouraging the same.

In 1903, Gopal Krishna significantly raised issues of spendthriftness on army, partialism in public rights and neglect of primary education. The Government was claiming that India was progressing under British rule. Gopal Krishna was exposing hollowness of this calm. He proved through data how the Government was overlooking primary education.

Gopal Krishna's full faith on debate based on facts and common public was also getting much influenced by his ideas. The Government was afraid of public opinion going against it and their reputation could be tarnished. Gopal Krishna was constantly striking the government on moral ground.

In 1904, budget speech, Gopal Krishna had attracted Government's attention to price inflation worrying over rupee deflation. He demanded to finish excise duty on cotton and decreasing cost of salt. Besides these, he demanded to curb land revenue tax in Bombay, Madras and North-West provinces. He told how people distressed by bad crops affected by famine might have to face heightened agony due to land revenue, using the facts. He demanded a total ban of wine sale mentioning common consumption of wine among poor.

Gopal Krishna had criticised railway policy of the Government in witness borne before Welby Commission. Repeating the same issue in budget speeches of 1906, he said, "In the last eight years, the Government has received a profit of more than 35 crores rupees and this entire amount has been burnt in the name of railway expansion. Apart from this amount, amount from another fund is also spent for railways." He said, "The Government was not paying attention to spend amount for basic needs of public." He had asked, "Is railway alone everything? Is public education not at all important?"

Gopal Krishna gave many suggestions to reduce government control on land, agricultural development, getting farmers' loan free, arrangements for irrigation, science-supported agriculture, development of industrial and technical education, primary education and sanitation derive. He entered political field from educational one and very well understood importance of education. He continuously used to protest Government's neglect of primary education. In 1907, Gopal Krishna felt pleased that the Government had reduced salt tax, accepting his demand. But while declaring rebate in salt tax, the finance member has made fun of poor people saying, "Poor of India are contributing to the Government treasure through salt tax only." Protesting this statement, Gopal Krishna said that the statement of finance member is untrue. Poor public is contributing through land revenue, sale of wine, excise duty on cotton, registration fees, forest fees, etc. to the Government treasury. Poor public has not to pay only income tax.

In budget speech, Gopal Krishna suggested that there was a need to show income and expenditure account of railway separately. His suggestion was accepted. He also demanded to show irrigation tax also separately but this demand was not accepted. The Government got ready to curb out military expenditure a little and agreed to spend a little more on primary education. This could be possible due to powerful protest by Gopal Krishna.

Year 1909 arrived with a message of change. The age of profit budget was about to end now. It was also the last year of old legislation. Very next year, Minto-Morley Reforms were set to be regulated. In his budget speech, Gopal Krishna had also thrown light on political affairs. Nine patriots of Bengal were exiled on the basis of law of the year 1818. He demanded the government to set them free. He also discussed 'Reforms Act'. The point of conferring representation to Muslims was said in this Act. Gopal

Krishna was against any type of favouritism or discrimination in the name of caste or religion.

In 1911, Gopal Krishna was allotted time 20 minutes only to comment on budget. He threw light over Burma's financial system and relation between provincial and imperial councils. He told it necessary for certain essential rules to be followed by provinces before they were awarded the right of tax.

The 1912 speech of Gopal Krishna was very brief. He advised Government to appoint a Commission to find out measures for revenue increase.

Gopal Krishna was called 'leader of opposition party' owing to his role played as an extraordinary public well-wisher leader in the imperial legislative council.

□

15

Establishment of Servants of Indian Society

Gopal Krishna has presented an important gift to his country in the form of 'Servants of India Society'. He believed that this country needs devoted and capable workers, who could devote their life to the service of their nation. He had established Servants of India Society to materialise his second assumption.

The assumption of public service was not propagated in true sense in India before the British rule. Christian missionaries had presented example of public service by establishing schools and hospitals. Enough progress was made in the field of public service through this effort. But it was assumed among people that social welfare devotion of missionaries was aimed to run their religion conversion campaign only. The emotion of social service was not infused in the country. Same type of neutral atmosphere was prevailing in political scenario also. People of India were entering politics without sufficient knowledge and grasp on problems. The need was felt that building of workers, devoted to public service to remove pain and sorrow of society's lower classes. Several public organisations of Pune were active keeping this view only in their conscious. The beginning of welfare work had already taken place. But lack of dedicated workers in the field of politics and economic policies was being experienced. There was need to work meaningfully to unite people.

On 12 June, 1905, Shiv Rai, Hari Sathe, the ex-colleague of Gopal Krishna from Sarvajanik Sabha, had laid foundation stone of Servants of India Society at Pune. Workers of Samiti took oath of public service. This was a day of joy for Gopal Krishna. First of all, he himself took oath, then Natesh Appaji Dravid, Anant Vinayak Patwardhan and G.K. Deodhar took oath to take country as supreme and to continue service for national welfare. They will never think of personal profit or advantages while serving the nation. They will serve without any discrimination taking all the Indians as their siblings; they will also develop same emotion of equality in their own family. They will not spend their energy to earn for themselves and will keep on passing completely ideal life, will not quarrel with someone, will always take care of social interest, will not conduct themselves in a manner contrary to society's ideals.

Gopal Krishna believed, while forming the society, it will be possible to prepare powerful structure after removing initial hiccups. In the preface of society's legislation, gratitude was expressed to British influence as useful in favour of Indian interests. Special emphasis was paid on conduct and capacity-building in constitution. It was said in it: "Public life should be certainly spiritual. Every heart should have patriotic emotion. Boundless patriotism should be there to sacrifice everything. Minds should have courage to stay indauntable towards ideals. Workers must be totally dedicated for nation's service". Ideals of this type only were fixed.

Gopal Krishna was made of clay of patriotism and wanted to build his society likewise. Here it will be relevant to mention that Gandhiji had also chosen ideals somewhat resembling while establishing Ashrams and he himself wanted to become a member of society. Gandhiji used to praise Gopal Krishna often for connecting spiritualism to politics and also used to try these ideals to turn/infuse into his practical life.

Gopal Krishna has sent copies of rules manual of society legislature to Ferozshah Mehta and principal Selby, etc. prestigious and recognised persons. Selby was principal of a college at Pune. He was a member of Fergusson College managing committee at Pune and an admirer of Gopal Krishna. He suggested Gopal Krishna that it was not proper to annex the word 'secret' with legislation. Gopal Krishna corrected this.

Founding Servants of India Society was an important incident of history of prevailing India in spite of its difference of opinions and objections. It makes clear the extent to which Gopal Krishna was a constructive thinker. Even if all of his lectures, writings and political works are forgotten, even then, just for establishing Servants of India Society, the country will always keep on remembering him with respect. The society became successful with time to play an important role. The society that was established to serve the country.

Servants of India Society had turned into a sort of post-graduate institution where training members used to study daily life's bitter reality, used to come in contact of people, used to understand problems well and used to face foreign rule in a legal manner. If the members earned good on being highly posted, then they used to deposit rest of amount except keeping some for fulfilling their basic needs.

This society moving ahead with such great ideals played an exemplary role in national welfare. Its members worked in movements of tribals and labour unions. This society played special role in eradicating discrimination meted out to Indians. For this, society also worked in foreign countries. Society also kept on playing praiseworthy role in providing relief to floods, famine, epidemics, and earthquake-affected people. Society also contributed specially in propagating and promoting education among females. Society also formed co-operative societies for economic progress of lower classes in society. The persons attached with society, like Shri Niwas Shastri, Thakkar Bapa, N.M. Joshi, G.K. Deodhar, S.G. Waje,

H.N. Kunjak, Kondana Rav, K.G. Vibhaye, Bakhane and A.D. Mani can be named as sources of pride to any nation.

Society had branches at Bombay, Nagpur, Madras and Allahabad apart from headquarters at Pune. In the society's head office, 'Gokhale School of Politics and Economics', was established.

Gopal Krishna had not to stop any project in lack of finances. This prestige as member of Imperial Legislative Council had grown and his image as devoted public leader was already established. He could arrange the amount according to need. Few rich persons would have presented him blank cheques for society demands. But he never took undue advantage of the generosity of donors. He wanted to prove that lack of funds is never an obstacle in virtuous deeds.

In this context, it can be mentioned that in 1905, Gopal Krishna was collecting funds to construct Ranade's memorial also. Approximately, one lakh rupees were collected for this activity. Gopal Krishna wanted to establish 'Ranade Economic Institute'. His dream was taking shape. In 1910, this institute was inaugurated and which was conducted by Pune University later on.

Establishing Servants of India Society was heartily welcomed by public and intellectual section. On the other hand, bureaucrats had doubts regarding its future. Contemporary finance member, Sir May Fleetwood Wilson had written a letter on 2 September, 1910 from Shimla – "On date 19, I spent several hours with Mr. Gokhale and members of Servants of India Society. Building of college is of superior quality. Library is very fine and whole of arrangement is very well organised. Sanitation is taken full care of the members I met, were aged in span of twenty to thirty years. I got highly impressed after meeting them. I talked with them at length. I also conversed with Mr. Gokhale. In spite of this, I could not understand clearly what is the basic aim of establishing this society? Entire plan appears to be based on hypothesis and I am afraid of those young men appearing in search of government or municipality services. They are highly educated and can be better public servants."

□

16

From the Post of Congress Secretary to Congress President

Gopal Krishna was being neglected in Congress after apology episode. In 1897 Amravati Session of Congress, neither he was permitted to sit on stage with distinguished leaders nor he was invited to lecture or to present any proposal. He had decided not to initiate from his own will till Congress did not come to feel his need. He faced this bad period with his patience and discipline. After this in 1904, he was elected Congress secretary. Then he continuously kept on becoming an important personality for Congress.

Probably, after the storm raised by Congress division, Congress' point of view underwent a change. Gopal Krishna was in direct contact of the British Government in India and England and Congress leaders had thought that Congress could be aided by his contacts. Even if decision of portion could not be altered, its ill-effects could be surely reduced. The second point was that leadership wanted to keep liberal camp unified.

At the end of year 1904, in annual session of Congress at Bombay, Sir William Wedder Burn presented a proposal that all the representatives of all the Indian provinces be sent to England on a tour where next year General Elections were to be held. These representatives could try to prepare public opinion. Only Gopal Krishna and Lala Lajpat Rai could go on England tour. After few months of establishing Servants of India Society and days before Bengal partition's declaration. On 16 September, 1905, Gopal Krishna set off for England from India. He stayed at England for fifty days.

Both the leaders had such quality that could be termed complimentary to each other. On one hand, Lajpat Rai was addressing public as a powerful orator and on the other hand, Gopal Krishna had addressed forty-five meetings in a span of fifty days. Daily he kept on working for eighteen hours each. His health had deteriorated due to continued tension and his throat had to be operated upon at the time of return to motherland.

It is a separate issue if voting in England was influenced through his lectures. But this was the fact that he had represented India's view powerfully. He clarified few more points; for example, Congress wanted to boycott English-made clothes in India. Gopal Krishna wanted to inform Manchester labourers also along other citizens. He told Manchester labourers not to get displeased with India but should be displeased with people, who partitioned Bengal. Indians had become frustrated with this decision and they had no way left/open except to boycott foreign cloth. People had listened his lectures. Attentively, his words influenced English deeply. Wedderburn had suggested to establish dialogue with British voters. This had proved an effective measure.

Apart from presenting India side accurately, Gopal Krishna had contributed in strengthening economic aspects of Congress journal *India* being published from England. This journal was occurring loss at that moment. Gopal Krishna had been successful in turning people into customers for the journal.

Gopal Krishna had returned India on 5 September, 1905. It was an amazing fact that a welcome function was organised at Bombay by presidency association for his services (felicitation) at England. President of Association, Sir Ferozshah Mehta and his colleagues had not arrived to welcome Gopal Krishna. What could have been the reason behind it? It was clear through prevailing incidents that Mehta was not happy with Gopal Krishna. He had not liked the decision to establish Servants of India Society and so Mehta neglected Gopal Krishna on this point only? In 1905, Mehta had not involved himself in Banaras session of Congress also, which was chaired by Gopal Krishna who had himself sent invitation for Mehta to attend.

But one more leader, who was considered from opposition camp, introduced his good wishes, thus Tilak welcomed Gopal Krishna with enthusiasm and warmth. A public meeting was organised at Pune where Tilak had thanked Gopal Krishna to perform in favour of India's interest. Through proposal, Tilak and Gopal Krishna did not like to even spare a glance on each other on few occasions. But Bengal partition brought them close. Tilak had even got coloured pictures of Gopal Krishna distributed alongwith his own newspaper *Kesri* and *Maharatta* among readers. Tilak had shown that it was possible to establish rapport and good heartedness even in public life.

One more honour was awaiting Gopal Krishna. In September 1905, while he was leaving for England, meanwhile he was informed that he could be elected president of the next session of Congress. He had requested the managing committee that his age was only forty years and he was not ready to carry this responsibility at such an age immature for the post. But Congress leaders were well aware of their decision being correct. They wanted to hand-over boat of Congress to a trustworthy sailor of this type during times of storm. They considered Gopal Krishna perfectly fit for the post of president. Gopal Krishna had a balanced point of view, sober personality and sufficient experience of nation's service. There could be no person better than himself for the post of party president.

Gopal Krishna had many challenges ahead. The dormant nationalism in India had been awakened by Curzon's decision of Bengal partition. The maximum turbulence was taking on in Bengal. After this, the historical struggle that went on in, is familiar to all. Curzon got highly annoyed due to emergence of revolt in Bengal against British rule. He wanted to divide nationalistic powers into pieces. He had wanted to isolate Muslim elements from 'unified front'. Muslims were in majority in east Bengal. He had wanted to divide and rule and he was a great expert of this skill. Though argument given after partition that it had become difficult to rule such a large area from administrative point of view. But in reality, partition was a result of political conspiracy.

A strong reaction was felt in Bengal. Approximately, 500 public meetings were arranged against Bengal partition. To annule/repeal decision of partition, a memorandum with signatures of sixty thousand people was sent to England. At that time, Lord Curzon decided to resign due to rifting his opinion with Army Chief of India, Lord Kitchner. But before resigning from his post, he had a desire to conclude decision of partition. In August 1905, at Shimla session of Imperial Legislative Council was organised, where included Government servants only, Curzon got Bengal Partition Act passed. This Act was to be effective from October 1905. There was a sharp reaction among people. Bengal drowned in grief and mourning the day this 'Act' was regulated.

In this environment only, Banaras session of Congress had been arranged. A great number of representatives came to join session. How could Gopal Krishna show the citizens path during such a moment of crisis? Presidential lecture of Gopal Krishna was brilliant and guiding. He criticised Lord Curzon's regime, welcoming Prince and Princess of Wales and new Viceroy Lord Minto in India. He compared Curzon's rule to the rule of Aurangzeb. In both the rules, power was centered in hands of one person only. Lord Curzon possessed few of other qualities but he could not understand Indian people's emotions properly as he was not sensitive at all. He never used to have faith on principles of freedom under human development. He contributed in strengthening British rule in India and treated Indians like dumb animals. Gopal Krishna said that we would leave any hope of cooperation with bureaucracy in public interest, if public will be refuted like this and will be abandoned helpless on his condition. In this way, Gopal Krishna had predicted the conditions to appear soon, as Mahatma Gandhi had begun non-cooperation movement.

Gopal Krishna had expressed view on the issue of 'Swadeshi' and 'Boycott' also. According to him, Boycott was a political weapon, which should had been used in extraordinarily necessary circumstances only. This weapon could have proved useful for attracting ruler's attention towards public agony. He accepted it to be a constitutional and legal weapon. He said that one must inspect all the dangers before using this weapon and remove all the differences of ideas and opinions. He had asked to revive handloom industry, emphasising adoption of 'Swadeshi', which could provide some extra income to farmers. He told about hopes and ambitions of India, mentioning political field. He sharply criticised country's bureaucracy. He ended his lecture with statement of Ranade showing moral aspect of life, which said, "It is important and essential to sanctify and complete human consciousness to let it be free."

Apart from presidential lectures, there were few more proposals to be pondered upon. A delegation had come all the way from Bengal, fully grief in partition. This delegation wanted Congress to boycott India tour of Prince of Wales by passing a proposal. They also wanted to get proposal of boycotting British goods also. Traders got divided due to different opinions. Surendra Nath Bannerji was opposing both the proposals. Tilak did not want to boycott tour of Prince of Wales but was agreeable to boycott of British goods proposal. Before all this, Congress had already invited Prince of Wales to attend its session, which was not accepted by Prince. Congress was in a dilemma and the same dilemma kept on disturbing Gopal Krishna also. He demonstrated unique skill to remover this bottleneck. He requested Ramesh

Chandra Dutt to make Surendra Nath Bannerji agreeable to 'British goods boycott', proposal. Surendra Nath got agreed. After this, Tilak and Lajpat Rai needed to be agreed but his proposal of amendment was defeated in subject committee. Then he informed of current subject in open session. Gopal Krishna personally requested Lajpat Rai to stop pressurising for proposal 'Boycott of Prince'. Lajpat Rai got agreed. Now Tilak was left. Gopal Krishna got Lajpat Rai to make Tilak also agreeable; because only Lajpat Rai alone could make him agree. In this way, Gopal Krishna had obtained solution to remove bottleneck by introducing his wit.

□

17
Morley-Minto Reforms

Gopal Krishna had faith to find out solution of any matter on the basis of policy of dialogue. If he would have assisted in all the governmental programs, then he could have reached on a high and reputed post. Its example is the 'Companion of the Indian Emperor' (CIE) title he received. Perhaps he accepted this post only so that he must not appear as an obvious opponent of government. Also to prepare an environment where government could listen to his opinion attentively.

Besides being on post of president of one Congress session, he was so dear to government that it could not do without him. One section of Congress used to conduct him according to itself and government also desired to conduct him accordingly. He did not ever leave any of these companies. Even before partition of Congress at Surat, authority had been transferred in hands of liberal group. Already, extremist or non-liberal group was defeated in general election. Morley, the scholar of politics and philosophy, was appointed new Viceroy of India, which showed a ray of hope to India.

On 14 April, 1906, Gopal Krishna started off for Britain for the third time. It was an opportune moment to expose, Bengal excesses and torture to all and supporting political reforms. He had met with India minister and addressed few meetings. He caused a turbulence by putting forth deaths of two crore people occurred due to hunger in a span of ten years. Even at the prevailing time, seven crore people had no access to food properly. Death (mortality) rate was fast increasing in the country. He examined faulty policies of Lord Curzon.

The new governor of Bengal, Sir Bempfield Fuller exceeded all the limits to show his authority. He banned procession and meeting. Along with this, he tightened vigil on the students and teachers. Increasing indignation in people. Surendra Nath Bannerji was arrested along president and representatives on the occasion of Barisal provincial assembly. Everybody was fined ₹ 200 per head. In case of non-payment of fine, administration came down to opting insulting ways. Gopal Krishna put this matter also in front of British officers and alongside requested to get this issue examined.

Morley and Minto both got agreed with Gopal Krishna fully. They asked Fuller to clarify this matter. Meanwhile, Fuller ordered Calcutta University to derecognise Sirajganj High School as he got advice, due to incident of raising slogans of Vande Mataram there. Fuller did not become ready even on intervention of Lord Minto. Instead threatened to resign in case derecognition of the school was not undertaken. This threat was really welcomed and Lord Minto accepted Fuller's resignation immediately without any hesitation.

In these circumstances, Bengal bureaucracy became alert to abandon the process of crushing Bengal's public. It starred to adopt liberal policy towards public. The credit for this change goes to untiring efforts of Gopal Krishna. He took up many meetings with Morley to request governmental order of Bengal partition taken back. These meetings proved encouraging. Morley got ready for setting up a commission, which was to examine the extent of governmental cooperation with Indians, so that this cooperation could be enhanced according to the need. Besides this, Gopal Krishna also said that the discontent would remain till power was not handed over to Indians.

Public was grieved with Bengal partition by Lord Curzon, which had fastened the pace of revolutionary activities. Owing to ruling system being in party-hand and opinion difference with Army Chief Lord Kitchner, Curzon had left India after resignation. This way, Gopal Krishna received opportunity to make government agree for not using force. Lord Minto and India minister Marley had accepted this fact that Lord Curzon's administrative policies were all wrong. Morley started to satisfy nationalist elements. He wanted that generous attitude should be meted out to people so that their wrath gets pacified.

After 5-6 meetings with Morley, Gopal Krishna starred feeling that Morley was ready to take few positive steps in the favour and interest of India. This point made him write a letter to his friend Dravid that he should make Tilak understand to criticize Morley-Minto in his newpaper. He kept on fixing his target on actual enemies only. He had requested his friend Cathver in the same way.

Looking at Morley and Minto's letter exchange, it becomes obvious that they also considered Gopal Krishna as their great friend. In spite of this, Morley was not ready to confer self-rule (Home Rule) opportunity to Indian people. Owing to this, Gopal Krishna could not stop Morley's criticism being published in newspaper.

Morley said at one point in his lecture, "I could not gift Indian people the moon (freedom). Due to this reason only, people out there are quite angry with me because moon (freedom) is not in my hands and even if it was, I would not have given it."

In 1906, when Gopal Krishna returned from England the condition of country was serious for pondering. He could not have any special achievement in England. People were not satisfied with peaceful programme of liberal group in country. Public had inclined towards directly collision with regime by the people's groups.

A Muslim delegation under leadership of Agha Khan met Viceroy Lord Minto in October 1906 at Shimla and demanded to consider Muslim interest separately while decision about India was to be taken. Fuller had created a wall between Hindus and Muslims and in actuality, Fuller will be considered perpetuator of Pakistan. Jinnah and Muslim league erect a wall only after this foundation was laid.

Morley presented his plan for reforms on 2 June, 1907 in which declaration on establishing a royal commission to think over centralisation of power was made. The declaration of Morley's reforms could not spread any wave of pleasure in India.

Ramsay McDonald in his book 'The Awakening of India' has written: "The achievements made by All India Muslim League as soon as it was founded, was in practice, supported by English authorities. This type of doubt permeated India. Above-mentioned officers had sown the seed of partition in country by favouring Muslim League with particular kindness at Shimla."

Indian Reforms Act, 1906 could not fulfil aspirations of India, power kept on being contained in the hands of centre only. It was Minto's clear opinion. One should accept with blindfolded eyes, whatever government gives no change had taken place actually in government machinery. So, political leaders kept on rotting in prisons. The repressive policy of government kept on getting more aggressive.

□

18

Gopal Krishna Gokhale, Mahatma Gandhi and South Africa

Gopal Krishna had dedicated a large span of his life for Indians residing in South Africa. Mahatma Gandhi had said, "It is my belief if all the Indians put up a stiff opposition to Indian Transvaal Registration Act, then they will gain the supporting regard of Indians."

On one hand, Mahatma Gandhi got sentimental and, on the other hand, Gopal Krishna had also not remained indifferent to the same. Rather Mahatma Gandhi moved very close to Gopal Krishna while struggling with non-resident Indians at South Africa and he declared himself the pupil of Gopal Krishna Gokhale.

If we talk of other cases besides European ones, i.e. non-White South Africans, their life have been always miserable, White race always took Black Africans and their slaves and means of fulfilling their own interest. In 1795, England acquired authority over Cape of Good Hope. English people settled in Cape and seashore colonies of Natal and Africans succeeded in establishing two northern republics, namely Free State and Transvaal. After defeat of Africans in Boer War, this republic and colony were merged in that union, which was established in 1910. At that time, union had majority of English people.

In 1893, Mahatma Gandhi had already arrived in South India; one-and-half lakh of Indians had settled in Natal, after arriving from India up to that time. All of them were contractual labourers. There was no trouble till they kept on working. But after completion of work, they started pinching English and others. English people stated to apply many restrictions and humiliating conditions upon them. In 1888, Orange Free State stripped off Indians of all their rights. Indians were bound to pay 'three pound tax', for entry in Transvaal. In the year 1893, Whites imposed extra tax of twenty-five pounds on Blacks, which was supported by Viceroy Lord Elgin. During this period, much discussions of accident involving Gandhiji, i.e. his being thrown out to the station alongwith his luggage even after travelling with a ticket, paid for first class coach had taken place.

Mahatma Gandhi was desirous of practicing law at Bombay High Court after returning from South Africa. Alongside he also wanted to undertake public welfare work with Gokhale but then he had to go back to South Africa.

In 1909 Lahore Congress session, Mahatma Gandhi described the plight of Indians, residing in South Africa. Then Gopal Krishna got restless to help non-resident Indians. He immediately put a proposal, "What is this passive protest agitation running in South Africa? Our nature is self-defensive and it has a tradition of fighting a war with self-power (i.e. power of soul), face torture of extreme aggressive conduct with self-agonisation. We face animality of human beings with divinity, of torture with self-consciousness, of injustice with faith and bad conduct with good conduct." Being influenced with Gokhale's high ideology, Mahatma Gandhi had accepted him as his Guru.

Even Gopal Krishna was no less influenced by Gandhiji. He had said, "This is extremely good fortune of my life that I know Mahatma Gandhi very well. Gandhiji is among those people who are simple hearted, leading a disciplined life, followers of the highest principles of justice and truth. I can say unhesitantly that Indian individuals have searched it up to its high level in his form."

At Lahore Congress session, Gopal Krishna's lecture in relation to South Africa brought this effect that people showered money, silver, gold and ornaments to help Indians' struggle in South Africa. Industrialist Tata also sent twenty-five thousand rupees to Gandhiji, Nizam also sent two thousand rupees, Agha Khan collected three thousand rupees during Muslim League session.

On 25 February, 1910, in the Imperial Legislative Council, Gopal Krishna demanded immediate ban on contractual labourers being sent to Natal issue, which was accepted by the government. Later, Lord Amtihic and South African committee demanded to repeal condemnable acts of 1907. Under above-mentioned circumstances, African government passed a legislation on 11 February, 1911, but Indians did not get satisfied with it. Gandhiji expressed his protest of this legislation.

Gopal Krishna decided to travel South Africa following Mahatma Gandhi's request. He was in England at that time. He informed Mahatma Gandhi of his own arrival in South Africa. Mahatma Gandhi felt very happy receiving this news.

On 22 October, 1912, Gopal Krishna arrived Capetown. Union government welcomed him heartily and arranged a comfortable railway saloon for him. At that moment, it appeared as if whites were competing with Indians to welcome Gopal Krishna. A senior officer of migration department, Mr. Ruskin was appointed for his entire journey of South Africa. Hundred of Indians heartily welcomed Gopal Krishna and a huge procession was taken out to honour him, in which 50 cars were also included. Not only Indians but Europeans were also sufficiently impressed with lecture of Gopal Krishna.

He went from the Capetown to Johannesburg where Satyagraha was going on. Whites participated in large number in the function organised there. Mayor heartily greeted Gopal Krishna. After this, he was taken in a Government car to office venue, specially opened for him, where he could meet and interact with people, could do his work. Mahatma Gandhi worked on capacity of his secretary all through Gokhale's journey.

In-between this journey, Gopal Krishna organised a 'Bhoj', which included 150 Whites among 400 of invited guests. This was the first occasion of majority in lives of whites when an Indian had invited them for a 'Bhoj'. His lecture delivered at this occasion also proved effective emotions. Love, clarity and determination were infused in this lecture.

He had to face a strong dilemma in a meeting organised at town of which language should he speak in (address), because it was non-referential/irrelevant to speak in English. He could not speak in Hindi fluently. Later, on Gandhji's suggestions, Gopal Krishna delivered his lecture in Marathi, which was translated in Hindi by Mahatma Gandhi. In the same manner, Mahatma Gandhi translated Gopal Krishna's Marathi lectures in Hindi from Johannesburg to Zanzibar, while he never knew Marathi. Gopal Krishna also asked how he could translated his lecture into Marathi without being familiar with it? Gandhiji answered that he did not know Marathi but I understand everything said in favour of public interest. Emotion of public interest is not dependent on any language. It is such an emotion emerging from heart that anybody can easily understand. Gopal Krishna was deeply impressed with this answer of Gandhiji. He started looking at Gandhiji's future as very bright. On the other hand, Gandhiji was also very happy with the act that miles away from India, in South Africa where Indians are struggling for an aim, an Indian language only was relied upon.

Gopal Krishna, on arriving Pretoria from Natal, accepted hostship of General Smitts and General Botha and said what he wanted to. As was the quality of Gopal Krishna, he always remained correct, even in very trivial statements even. Gandhiji prepared draft of this dialogue. On 15 November, talks were started in a friendly environment. Whole and sole promises were made in this conversation. Assurance of curbing bottleneck in migratory laws and three pounds tax were given during talks. But Mahatma Gandhi was very well aware of the reality of these promises.

Before going to Pretoria, Gopal Krishna stayed in Tolstoy Farm established by Gandhiji from 2 to 4 November, where Gandhiji acted as his personal assistant besides being his personal secretary. He himself cooked food for Gopal Krishna, washed his clothes. Gopal Krishna got very impressed with environment at Tolstoy Farm, its simple life, education being imparted to children, affection towards Gandhiji already present in his heart increased much more.

On 17 November, Gopal Krishna returned India via sea route. On every port on the way, he received a grand welcome. Gopal Krishna wanted Gandhiji also to accompany him to India, leaving South Africa and hold reins of freedom struggle.

Central officers of Africa broke their promise, made to Gopal Krishna. Gandhiji knew this fact beforehand. But Gopal Krishna had to face criticism by Ferozshah Mehta and Wacha as soon as he arrived to Bombay. They criticised Gopal Krishna for this so-called pact. In spite of this, pact between Gopal Krishna and South Africa was passed in Congress session.

Few days after this pact, Supreme Court gave its verdict that marriages of migrated Indians (to South Africa) ceremonised from South Africa only were illegal. In that condition, their wives, married in India, would not be able to step on South African land. A Muslim's married wife was asked to move out to South Africa. Women started Satyagraha to protest against this.

Government appointed a commission to solve this issue. In this situation, Gopal Krishna advised Gandhiji to finish his struggle at South Africa. Gandhiji explained his plea as an answer to Gokhale's advice.

Gandhiji sought blessings of Gopal Krishna's blessings to complete his work. Gopal Krishna blessed him in spite of few disagreements on many issues and also complete cooperation. He got full aid supplied to Gandhiji through Ramsay MacDonald, Valentine Creole and Indian Princes.

On 12 January, 1914, a pact was finalised between Mahatma Gandhi and General Karan. Benzamin Takeeson Commission could not get full cooperation of Indians. Later on, recommendations of commission were accepted. It was absorbed in 'Indian Relief Legislation' in which termination of three pounds tax accepting marriages legal in India as legal in South Africa also, was done on 26 June, 1914. This legislation was passed with 64 votes against 24 votes.

□

19

The Last Phase

Gopal Krishna went to England and returned to India on 20 November, 1914. It was his seventh and the last, sojourn to England. He went to England, being a member of public service commission, to participate in its public meeting. His health was deteriorated to the extent that doctors in England estimated that he could not survive for more than three years. He did not get upset hearing this statement of doctors, and kept on doing his work with cool mind.

On his return to India, Mahatma Gandhi went to visit (Gopal Krishna) at Pune. Mahatma Gandhi said in an interview to press: "At this present time, as Gopal Krishnaji has advised me perfectly, I cannot form a definite idea to issues related with Indians owing to my long absence in India. I must pass some time here as observer and learner. I have promised thus and I believe that I will fulfil my promise." In this way, he indicated that he has decided to serve motherland lifelong through his stay in India.

Gopal Krishna wanted Gandhiji to join Servants of India Society. Gandhiji also desired the same. But life members of the society were not in favour of this. They believed that ideals of society were not similar to Gandhiji's ideals and working style. Therefore, it was not proper of his immediate inclusion in the society. Consoling Gandhiji, Gopal Krishna said, "I hope they will accept you but if they do not do so, you must not think even for a moment that they have no feeling of respect or attachment for you in their heart. They do not want to take any type of risk. But whether you become its member or not, I will keep on considering you as its one part only." Gandhiji was deeply influenced with these words.

Gandhiji returned India carrying along members of Phoenix Ashram with him and wanted to establish an Ashram. Gopal Krishna put a well-wishing proposal before him. Whatever result comes out of your talks with members, I will give you funds to establish 'Ashram' and I will also consider this Ashram as my own only. He directed one of his colleagues to open an account after Gandhiji's name and take funds necessary for establishing Ashram, available only.

It was Gopal Krishna's generous nature only which mesmerised Gandhiji to compare him with the 'Ganges'. Gandhiji had toured Shanti Niketan after sojourn of Pune. After Gandhiji's arrival there, he received news of Gokhale's demise. He considered Gopal Krishna as his Guru. In a 'mourning meeting', Gandhiji had said, "I was in search of a true leader and I got only one such leader in the entire country. Gopal Krishna was that very leader." Mahatma Gandhiji decided to walk barefoot for one year to honour his Guru. He arrived Pune on 22 February. Now, he was determined to join Servants of India Society. When Gopal Krishna was alive, there was no need for Mahatma Gandhiji to receive membership. Now he was considering being a member as his prime duty.

There was quite a difference in ideas and opinions among society members. Long discussions took place and in the end, they took a decision that could be said justful or correct towards Gokhale's memory and unique personality of Gandhiji. They said, "After enough exchange of ideas, keeping different ideas, Gandhiji's point of view and aim of Gopal Krishna in mind, we have arrived to the conclusion that Gandhiji should travel to India upto one year. According to rule 17, if society before opting for membership of society." This type of decision was made hard to everybody to know of sharp difference among members. Then he decided to take back his application for membership. Doing so, he believed that he was expressing his concern for the society and to his Guru. He had said in a letter written to president of society, Shri Niwas Shastri – "I have become a true member of society by taking back my membership application." He meant that he will keep being devoted to Gopal Krishna's aim.

Till the time of death of Gopal Krishna, his assignment of Public Service Commission, Congress had continuously kept demanding that discrimination between Europeans and Indians in the field of public service should be ended. The commission was appointed under the pressure of this demand, only Gopal Krishna used to attempt to get constitutional recognition to this claim of Indians.

Through his budget speeches also, he had expressed protest in his witness, admitted before Welby Commission, that Indians were not being appointed on high posts. On 17 March, 1911, N. Subba Rao Puntoolu had presented a proposal in Imperial Legislative Council, to appoint a commission for looking into issue of appointments of Indians on high posts of civil administration. Gopal Krishna had supported the proposal but Government was postponing matter of intelligence in Indians. So, they must not be appointed on high posts. Gopal Krishna used to ask questions patiently and intelligently. At night, he used to write his opinion on written coitnesses, so that no protesting witness could ill-influence. This work was so challenging that perhaps a thinker and ideologist of Gopal Krishna's cadre alone could complete and materialise it.

Gopal Krishna did not stay active upto the completion of commission task. Had he been alive, commissioner's report could not have been dissatisfactory. But daily routine of working 20-20 hours per day made his health deteriorate and he died an untimely death. It is said that his struggle to gain Indian's rights at South Africa snatched ten years of his life and rest of ten years were snatched by public service commission's task.

Chaubal was not agreeable to the conclusion of commission but he had signed on the report of commission, given by majority. He was member of executive committee of the Bombay Government. Madras High Court Judge Abdur Rahim had shown courage disagreeing and writing his report separately. Contribution of Gopal Krishna was remembered in reports of majority and minority groups each. It was written in report by majority – "He was running sick since last few months, in spite of this, he had participated with self-determined power and dedication in our proceedings. We are benefited with the experience he gained through service of nation and we believe that we have tried to reflect his feelings in our report."

Abdur Rahim wrote in his report – "He had studied queries related to public services in this country with his dedication, foresight and the main proposal I am presenting. I believe that he would have expressed his support. Be it understood that I have prepared this proposal after consulting him."

After a few days, Abdur Rahim unveiled statue of Gopal Krishna at Madras. Expressing his reverence, he had said – "I have met him a little less and was not known to him well. But it did not take me excess of time to understand according to his character and intelligence what great person was he. Actually, whenever he asked a question, then it became difficult for anyone to answer him. He used to take special care of his facts and had full information of his subject. That is why, it was difficult for anyone to answer him or tackle his arguments."

The Government had appointed Esselington Commission without care and its suggestions were not even followed properly. Its objective was not to fix participation of local people in administration of India but only Government's will to avoid any hassle of agitation near about king's visit. It was past one year of world war when report was presented, so that it could not attract attention of public. In these circumstances, Indians' belief that commission's report will remain contained in file were being proved correct.

But attitude of British Government towards India had undergone a little change due to reason of war. It became imperative for rulers to gather India's support for strengthening defence procedure. In this context, role of Bombay Governor Lord Willingdon can be mentioned, who had a liberal point of view. After breaking of war, Willingdon has said, "Government should attempt something in this direction." In 1915, Lord Willingdon said, "British leaders should not await till India himself acquires political progress."

As the time prevailing, Gopal Krishna was present on the scenario and it was natural for him to take Gokhale's advice about minimum reforms to satisfy India. Lord Willingdon believed that any such proposal of Gokhale could be accepted by the Government, as its own proposal. This matter was kept in total secrecy. Willingdon's assumption behind Gopal Krishna's selection was that he understood limits of consultation very well and British leaders also had full faith on him. It was also possible for the ruling class to use Lord Willingdon as mediator. Gopal Krishna was not worried of hidden enemies behind proposals but he was not ready to accept this difficult challenge without the support of first order public leaders of India.

Gopal Krishna's worry was correct. If Indian leaders came to know of this proposal being prepared by Gopal Krishna, they could have refused to accept the same. This was the reason why Gopal Krishna told Lord Willingdon that he must get liberty/concession of consulting Sir Ferozshah Mehta and Sir Agha Khan. Willingdon agreed to grant this permission.

Gopal Krishna could not go to Bombay due to his deteriorating health. It could have been against dignity of both of the leaders, if they were called to visit Pune for this errand. But, at last, both of them were invited to Pune so that discussion at a very important political issue could be undertaken along with Gopal Krishna. But before fixed date of meeting, Gopal Krishna started experiencing an instinct of his last final hour of departure near. Unaware of his deteriorating health, Lord Willingdon reminded him of matter. It was incident of Wednesday. On Friday, Gopal Krishna renounced his physical and worldly existence.

After his death, one copy of proforma presented by him was given to Lord Willingdon, Ferozshah Mehta and Sir Agha Khan each.

It was a secret document which was made public in August 1917 at a time when Montagu declared reforms. Sir Agha Khan got his draft in England and Shri Niwas Shastri got it published in India.

□

20

The Demise

The lost moments were approaching fast. Gopal Krishna was warned in England only that he won't be able to survive for long. He wanted to serve his country till the last breath. Once an idea of turning ahead crossed his mind and a feeling towards material world kept on growing in his mind. He was awaiting DEATH like Ravindra Nath Tagore described it in his book *Gitanjali* – "As a bride is awaiting her bridegroom." He did not opt for meditation and assumption. Neither he worshipped God as a symbol nor used to go on pilgrimages. But a spiritual angle of view for daily routine of life, owing to which he used to stay cool minded in each and every condition.

On 13 February, 1915, when Mahatma Gandhi was being welcomed in society, Gopal Krishna got fainted and could not attend the programme. After getting conscious, he started his work even after feeling weakness. Till date 17, he was preparing letters and important documents or was getting some important things written through his dictation. He desired to prepare and present draft of Indian constitution and legislation to Lord Willingdon. He wrote letters to many friends on Thursday in his troublesome condition only. His health kept on deteriorating on Friday morning. Even in that trying time, he completed work of writing draft of constitution. He had kept on writing firmly with pencil. This was his last of the great efforts to serve India. He also wanted to complete public service commission's assignment but got disappointed when not being able to do so.

Friday morning, shadow of the death had started hovering over him. One member of society, Dr. Dev had left any hope of his survival and called other prominent doctors, V.C. Gokhale and Shikare for treatment. Even both of them could not locate any ray of hope. At that moment, Gopal Krishna was conscious and did not want visiting of other specialist doctors. He was also not in favour of issuing any bulletin about his health. He wanted to embrace death peacefully.

He called sisters and daughters to him and asked them to keep patience and not to shed tears. He also informed them of arrangement for their future. He forbade society members adieu and talked to his employees, specially the cook. He made one of the society members, Vasan Rao Patwardhan near him and said emotionally, "Many times I have talked harshly with you. Excuse me." At this, Patwardhan's eyes got filled with tears. Again Gopal Krishna asked him if Vasan had excused him. Then word came out of Patwardhan's mouth 'Yes'. Dr. Dev and famous Marathi novelist H.N. Apte were sitting beside him. Gopal Krishna addressed Apte: "I had seen only bright side of life upto now, I am about to look at its other side now."

Now he was feeling that moment to depart had arrived. He was attached to cleanliness and civility, soberity. He had worn *dhoti* and shirt. He wanted to get seated in his favourite chair. After some time, he gestured towards sky with his finger. After this, he joined his hands (in pose of 'namaskar' – the Indian greeting). In such a manner, he died with calm and peace. At that time, it was 10:25 pm, stars were twinkling in the sky and silence was prevailing all around. But it was matter of a very little time that the news of his death broadcasted all around the city, all over the nation. A sensation of loss, grief and mourning propagated at the untimely demise of such a great leader. Contemporary of Gopal Krishna, Lokmanya Tilak had gone to 'Singbad' for rest-care due to his failing health. He was sent a message to come back.

Mourning overshadowed society compound of the members, friends and admirers of late national leader had flooded to pay their homage. A huge procession was taken out, which passed through main roads of the city. Whole of the city was mourning. People crowed both the sides of roads; people were offering floral tributes to him. Procession reached there and Tilak had arrived at this occasion. Intellectual and social reformer Dr. R.G Bhandarkar, Principal, Fergusson College Dr. R.P. Paranjpe, and Tilak expressed the words felt by their heart's core. Emotions, appreciation and agony were infused in Tilak's statement. He said, "This is the moment of shedding tears. Today diamond of India, crown of Maharashtra, prince of workers is lying on the bed. Look at him and pay floral tributes. All of you should look upto his life like a standard to be followed. You should try to fill the lacuna created by his death. If you will try to continue his objectives, then his soul will certainly find peace."

Condolence messages started pouring in from all over the world and condolence meetings were organised place-to-place. Newspapers published obituaries for him. Many reputed and recognised persons like George V, Viceroy Lord Hardinge, Secretary of State, Governors of Bombay, Madras and Bengal, Nawab of Rampur, Maharajas of Banaras and Bhavnagar had sent their condolence messages.

On 3 March, a condolence meeting was held at Pune. The meeting was chaired by Bombay Governor, Lord Willingdon. Mahatma Gandhi presented proposal of condolence in the meeting. On this occasion, even Agha Khan was among the speakers. A condolence meeting was organised at Bombay also. A decision to build a memorial monument was made in the memory of Gopal Krishna.

□

21

Glimpses of the Life of Gopal Krishna Gokhale

Sarojini Naidu was admirer of Gopal Krishna. She had written an article titled "Gokhale – The Man" after his death, which, no doubt, contained unforgettable memories connected to Gokhale but light was also thrown on his personality, works and achievements.

Indian Nightingale, Sarojini Naidu wrote, "Entire world is quite familiar with his external personality and looks up to it with reverence. He had many special qualities – political analysis, his unparalleled tolerance for synthesis, his straightforward (merciless) impeccable expertise in matters of facts, his civil but indomitable plain speaking at the moment of a protest or opposition, his exemplary foresight, unparallel grace and courage to settle the issues honourably expanded political vision, discipline, vigorous voice, truthfulness in daily life, simplicity and sacrifice."

Sarojini Naidu had mentioned her own meetings with Gopal Krishna at Calcutta session of Congress in 1911:

Gokhale asked, "What is your opinion about India?"

Sarojini Naidu answered, "Future of India is hopeful."

"What do you think about its near future?" "Hindu-Muslim unity in a span of lesser than five years."

Gokhale said in an affectionate tone, "Child, you are a poetess, but you have expressed more of hope than expectations. This type of unity won't be established in my or your life span. Still, maintaining faith, keep on doing your job."

In March 1912, at Bombay, Sarojini Naidu met Gopal Krishna again. On meeting, he asked smiling, "Is there same flame in the torch still now?"

Sarojini Naidu said, "Much more than earlier."

Still Gopal Krishna was not appearing so optimistic for the same issue.

One session of Muslim League was held at Lucknow. Sarojini Naidu participated in it. A new legislation was passed in this session, which expressed a new emotion of cooperation in true manner with other communities for the first time, in all the matters of national welfare and progress.

That moment, Sarojini Naidu felt as if her dream has materialised. She visited Pune immediately and met Gopal Krishna. Those days Gopal Krishna was not keeping good health and he had become very weak.

Glancing at Sarojini Naidu, Gopal Krishna said, "Have you come to inform that your hypothesis had been proved true." After this, he asked about session from start to the last.

Sarojini Naidu has written, "At the moment, his face tired and wilted with pain, glittered producing a bright lustre of great joy, when I fully assured him that up to the matter of young people, they have extended their hand, not only with emotion of political propriety but inspired by real faith to the Hindus so obviously and generously."

Gokhale's answer was, "Till it is matter of our attitude, even it will always remain full of goodwill." After approximately one hour, I found him turning very tired owing to all this exuberance of emotions. At the evening time, I again met him. At that moment, I got to see his totally new face. This face possessed smartness and joy. But his face also had a palour. Even if there was not an iota of shade of grief, as was the case in the morning. Finding him advancing towards stairs, I shouted at him, "Are you thinking of climbing up all these steps?" He laughingly answered, "You have permeated a new hope in me. I have started feeling as if energy required to reface circumstances and being reactive has been sufficiently attained." Exactly at the same moment, his sister and daughters came to him. We kept on sitting for half-an-hour, in the balcony, wherefrom we could look easily at the setting sun. We kept on discussing current politics of country, along with appreciating the beautiful natural scene in front of us. It was the very first and lone occasion for me when I received a glimpse of that solitude-loving person's work-culture and family life. After departure of his daughters inside, we kept on sitting silently in twilight hours for long. After this, agitated by some deep mind force, Gokhaleji disturbed the silence to say so sincere the words as those of a sermon and enlightenment, whose influence has still now shadowed my heart. At that time, he told about honoured history and culture of India. He had said, "Stand near me! And in presence of these stars and mountains, taking these as witnesses. Devote your life, your intelligence, your voice, your music, you ideas and your hope and aspirations to motherland! You are a poetess. Taking inspiration from mountain tops, spread and convey message of hope, far and wide, to toiling public." On my asking his permission to bid him adieu, he said, "You have presented me a new hope, new confidence and new courage. Today, I will be able to sleep carefree."

After two months, Sarojini Naidu again met Gopal Krishna. She has written about that meeting, "On reaching London, there were both the known faces and faces unknown to me, among people welcoming me." Gokhale was also among them, who was in Western dress at that time. He had put a head on his head. I looked at him without batting an eyelid once and then asked, "Where is your that revolutionary cap gone?" Smiling, he took no note of my words. Gokhale had an all-likeable persona, which turned vocal while joining in the parties, theatre bridge and dining with ladies, on the terrace of liberal club. 'Cherry' was his great favourite. I constantly used to take care that wherever he might go, he must get cherries in sufficient quantity. I always used to joke with him, "There is always a cost of person. Your cost is few cherries."

Gopal Krishna's contemporary, Dr. Tej Bahadur Sapre, has mentioned an incident about him – "In 1907, Gokhale had visited North India to make people aware of proposals by Congress when he came to Allahabad, he did not allow anybody to visit him from ten o'clock in the morning to four o'clock in early evening, as he had to prepare his lecture during this time period. Twenty years had passed to his entry in active politics; still he prepared lectures taking enough pain. I attended this lecture. It was really a mesmerising lecture. I have never heard such a lecture on this topic anytime earlier."

Mahatma Gandhi has written about Gokhale, "Observing Gokhale's working style, the amount of please I drove equally the same extent of inspiration as well. There was no malignancy, non-responsibility, untruth ever seen in his words and matter. India's illiteracy and poverty always used to prick him like thorns. He had no answer to every visitor – You do this task and let me do mine. I have to gain independence for the country. Only after that, my attention will be diverted to other things. At this time, I have not even a moment's leisure."

"When Gokhale came to South Africa, our farm had nothing like a charpoy (cot). We begged and any how brought a cot for him in the Ashram, for Gokhale to sleep on it. There was no room, where he could have got total solitude. In this situation, how could healthwise delicate Gokhale get sufficient rest? Apart from this, farm was situated full one-and-half mile far away from the station. When I informed Gokhale of all these situations, then he expressed satisfaction over the entire arrangement. Unfortunately, it rained that night. Gokhale caught cold. I prepared special 'soup' for him.

Bhai Kotwal prepared hot and piping *chapatis* for him. It was difficult to keep food hot. Gokhale took this food without making faces. Finding us sleeping on floor Gokhale did not agree to sleep on the cot. He spread even his beddings also on the floor."

Pandit Jawaharlal Nehru has said, "I had attended Bankipur Congress session in the capacity of a representative. To a large extent, session was a great celebration of English-knowing high-class people. There, from morning to evening, people wearing freshly ironed clothes were seen roaming. Actually, this was like a social festival, which contained no political zeal in their hearts. Gokhale had arrived there straight from his South Africa journey. He was the main person in the session. He only, out of all the people gathered there, was appearing as one person to think with complete sincerity in political and public matters, owing to his brilliance, truthfulness and authority. He deeply influenced me."

When Gokhale came back from Bankipur Congress session, then an incident took place. Those days he was a member of public service commission. Owing to this reason, first class compartment was reserved for him. Gokhale wanted to travel alone in this compartment owing to his illness and solitude loving nature, so that he could get enough peace here as all where else, the train was jampacked with people. Bhupendra Nath Basu, who was of a very talkative nature, came to Gokhale's coach. He wanted Gokhale's permission to travel in his coach, which Gokhale granted even if unwillingly. After some time, Basu arrived with his two of the friends, who were as talkative as himself. For a long time, they kept on talking this or that useless things. Then they asked Gokhale, "If you sleep on upper berth, then it will be alright because I and my friends cannot have proper sleep on the upper berth" (as a habit). Then Gopal Krishna quietly moved to upper berth (without protesting).

Dr. Rajendra Prasad has written, "It is an incident of year 1910. A barrister friend informed me that Gokhale wanted to meet me. I was surprised to know this and I went to meet him. He said, 'May be one day, your advocacy practice may be roaring, you may earn a lot of money and may pass your life with great luxury but country has even some right over you. You are intelligent, that is why, this right is claimed more on you.'" Gokhale's words had impressed Rajendra Prasad in such a manner that he became a life member of Servants of India Society by swearing service to the nation.

□

Lifetime

1866: Birth in Kotluk village of Ratnagiri on 9 May
1879: Death of father
1880: First marriage
1881: Completion of Matriculation
1913: Sixth time journey of England
1882-84:
- College education: Received B.A. Degree
- Founded Deccan education society

1885:
- Established Fergusson College
- Appointed assistant teacher of New English School

1886: Life membership of Deccan Education Society
1887:
- Second marriage
- First meeting with M.G. Ranade

1888:
- Editorship of English section of *Sudharak*
- Selection as Secretary of 'Sarvajanik Sabha'
- Editor of quarterly magazine published by Sabha

1889: Participated in Bombay Session of Indian National Congress
1891: Appointed Secretary of Deccan Education Society
1893:
- Death of his mother
- Fund collection for Deccan Education Society

1895:
- Appointed as 'Joint Secretary' of Indian National Congress
- Fellowship of Bombay University
- Editorship of *Rashtra Sabha Samachar* journal

1896:
- Appointed Secretary of 'Sarvajanik Sabha
- Resignation from its magazine's editorship

- Founded Deccan Sabha
- First meeting with Mahatma Gandhi

1897:
- Maiden journey to England
- Sinew in front of Welby Commission
- Publication of Malaria eradication related Grievances (in England and malaria at Pune)
- First meeeting with John Morley
- Return from England
- Tender apology

1898: Bearing important role in Cholera Relief works.

1899:
- Elected member of Bombay Legislation Council
- His criticism of governmental remedies of famine relief

1901
- Protested land related laws
- Walk out from legislative council
- Opposition to include community-based principle in district municipality legislation
- Death of Ranade

1902:
- Retired from Fergusson College
- Selection as member of Imperial Legislative Council
- Delivery of maiden speech for budget

1903: One month stay of Mahatma Gandhi with Gokhale at Calcutta

1904: Conferred title of CIE, i.e. Companion of Indian Emperor

1905:
- Founded Servants of India Society on 12 June
- Chaired Banaras session of Indian National Congress
- Chairman of Pune Municipality
- Second Sojourn to England

1906: Third Sojourn to England

1907:
- Death of elder brother Govind
- Lectures at different places in North India
- Congress partition at Surat

1908:
- Hearing (Presentation) before Decentralisation Commission

- Fourth time travel to England
- Declaration of Morley-Minto Reforms
- Arrest of Tilak
- Defamation suit against 'Hindu Panch'
- Founding 'Ranade Economic Institute'

1910:
- Presentation of proposals related to Nantal Labourers (which was passed)
- Presentation of proposal for primary education which got rejected
- Criticism of Press Bill

1911:
- Presented basic education bill.
- Presented research paper on topic 'East and West' in Universal Races Congress'

1912:
- Presented his opinion for Bhupendra Nath Basu's proposal related to police administration in India
- Presented proposal regarding labourers
- Annulment of fundamental education bill
- Fifth time travel to England
- Went to South Africa and there meeting Gandhiji
- Appointment in Public Service Commission

1913:
- Sixth time journey of England
- Fund Collection for South Africa struggle

1914:
- Seventh Sojourn to England
- Refused proposal of KCIE
- Gandhi Smuts Pact
- Meeting with Gandhiji in London
- Failure of unity attempt of Congress

1915:
- Gandhiji's arrival
- Political will
- Death on 19 February

□□□